You've Got This: Learning to Let Go

By Sandra Lott

You've Got This: Learning to Let Go by Sandra Lott
Copyright © 2020. All rights reserved.

ALL RIGHTS RESERVED: No part of this book may be reproduced, stored, or transmitted, in any form, without the express and prior permission in writing of Pen It! Publications. This book may not be circulated in any form of binding or cover other than that in which it is currently published.

This book is licensed for your personal enjoyment only. All rights are reserved. Pen It! Publications does not grant you rights to resell or distribute this book without prior written consent of both Pen It! Publications and the copyright owner of this book. This book must not be copied, transferred, sold or distributed in any way.

Disclaimer: Neither Pen It! Publications, or our authors will be responsible for repercussions to anyone who utilizes the subject of this book for illegal, immoral or unethical use.

This is a work of fiction. The views expressed herein do not necessarily reflect that of the publisher.

This book or part thereof may not be reproduced in any form, stored in a retrieval system, or transmitted in any form by any means-electronic, mechanical, photocopy, recording or otherwise-without prior written consent of the publisher, except as provided by United States of America copyright law.

Published by Pen It! Publications, LLC
812-371-4128   www.penitpublications.com

ISBN: 978-1-952894-15-2
Edited by: Sue Fairchild
Cover Design by Donna Cook

Scripture references taken from The New King James Version

It's Time to Soar!

Learn to freefall into the Savior's hands by releasing your burdens to Him.

If you cannot do anything about it, then it is not meant for you.

"Praise be to the Lord, to God our Savior, who daily bears our burdens." (Psalm 68:19) NIV

Table of Contents

Introduction 1
   Chapter 1: The Unrest 7
   Chapter 2: The Roadblocks 15
   Chapter 3: Discovering the Cause 25
   Chapter 4: Who Do You Say I Am? God the Father 35
   Chapter 5: Jesus the Son 53
   Chapter 6: The Holy Spirit 63
   Chapter 7: Discovering Your Identity 75
   Chapter 8: Baby Steps 89
   Chapter 9: I Believe! Letting Go 99
   Chapter 10: Drinking from the Well 111
Epilogue 121
Special Invitation 126
Invitation to Salvation Prayer 127
GOD LOVES YOU! 129
Other Books by Sandra Lott 133
Children's Books 134

Introduction

I recently went to a fair with my husband and they had a Ferris wheel. Although it was not as big as some that I have seen, it was big enough! Even though I don't like heights, I went on the ride. Going up I was okay, but as soon as I reached the top, I froze. I had to close my eyes and hold on to my husband for dear life! As soon as I felt we had descended a bit, I opened my eyes and peace filled me again. As we moved around and around, I got tired of being afraid and wanted to see from the top. It was night and dark outside and I knew the lights from the city would be beautiful. So, when the cart we were in just happened to stop at the top, I finally worked up the nerve to open my eyes! Was it scary? Oh yes, it was scary at first, but as I sat there and looked around, I saw the beauty of the city lights at night.

When we give in to fear, worry, anxiety, and doubt we miss out on so much of what God has in store for us. How can He provide you with new things and do wonderful acts for you if you are still stuck in the past? Dare to step into the unknown and allow God to amaze you.

"I will bring the blind by a way they did not know; I will lead them in paths they have not known. I will make darkness light before them, And crooked places straight. These things I will do for them, And not forsake them" (Isaiah 42:16) NIV.

Holding onto the people or issues in your life you are worried about, and constantly trying to fix it yourself because you do not have the trust or patience to wait on God will not fix it. This is due to free will. Just because you want a person to change and you pray, witness, encourage, and love them, does not mean they will change. They must want to change. Worrying over them steals your joy, will not fix their problem, and will only prolong the outcome Gods wants for you which is peace in the middle of your storm and trust in Him.

"The Lord is not slack concerning His promise, as some count slackness, but is longsuffering toward us, not willing that any should perish but that all should come to repentance" (2 Peter 3:9).

Through the many issues of my life, it took me a long time to overcome fear. I had been hurt so much and for so long that I began to expect it. Without realizing what I was doing, I began to control things in my life. If I was sure in advance, I would not get hurt; I would go forward, but if I thought I would get hurt, I would try to fix by asserting choices for my desired outcome. This leaves God out totally.

My youngest son died in a car accident, which was one more thing that hurt me. Afterwards, I became very protective over my oldest son. He has had many issues of his own to work through due to the same abuse I also suffered from my ex-husband. So, when he began to decline in mental health, I feared losing him and often came to his rescue. Over time, it became a series of enabling circumstances. None of my interfering helped. Helping them is okay, but continually bailing them out of trouble is not helping, but enabling. I would bail him out every time he asked and the problem with that is, when he continually asked me, he was not reaching out to God. When you enable someone, all you are doing is helping them to stay comfortable in the pit they dug for themselves. We must stop that! Instead, each person needs to grow so uncomfortable and miserable in their pit that they finally cry out to God.

Years went by and, slowly, the Lord delivered me and opened my eyes to all the fear I had within and to the many issues that fear had caused me; issues that are family members like control, worry, and anxiety. These fears will also eventually invade your heart. I began to step out of my comfort zone and do things I had been afraid to do, and little by little, all the fear and it's family members dissipated.

In this book, you will discover the issues that are keeping you stuck and bound, afraid to let go and trust God. You will learn to ask yourself the important, "why's" behind every issue like, "Why do I feel this way, what is causing this feeling, and why do I act this way?" Discovering the cause and the answers to the why's is an important step to learning how to handle those feelings and actions in order to let go and trust God. If you are weighed down by the troubles surrounding you and you have not been able to move past them, then it is time you lay them down. Dare to lay them at the Savior's feet and watch and see what He will do.

"Cast your burden on the LORD, And He shall sustain you; He shall never permit the righteous to be moved" (Psalm 55:22).

In order to get past the roadblocks that keep you from trusting God, it takes determination and walking close to Him day by day. "Therefore, my beloved brethren, be steadfast, immovable, always abounding in the work of the Lord, knowing that your labor is not in vain in the Lord" (1 Corinthians 15:58).

You will arrive to the place where you can let go. You will get to the place when you stop trying to have everything all figured out. Take baby steps, one step at a time, and, as you do, you will experience God's faithfulness. Each time this happens it will grow your faith and help you to take more and more steps of faith. When you learn to let go completely, and let God stay in control, He will amaze you and His fruitful rivers will flow through you!

"He who believes in Me, as the Scripture has said, out of his heart will flow rivers of living water" (John 7:38).

At the Feet of My Savior

At the feet of my Savior is where I want to be.
Only in Him am I forever free!

At the feet of my Savior is where I want to be.
Only in Him my heart is filled with joy and peace eternally.

At the feet of my Savior I'll live out my days.
Trials come and go with tears of sorrow and tears of joy.
Heartaches on the inside, struggles on the outside, but even so,
at the feet of my Savior is where I long to stay.

Trials come and go, but my Savior's love and peace is in my heart to stay. I have my ups and downs, but Jesus loves me anyway. His grace is always there, every day.
So, at the feet of my Savior is where I'll stay.

At the feet of my Savior is where I want to be! He loves unconditionally!
Only in Him salvation has come! Only in Him my battles are won!
Only in Him I'll live eternally! At the feet of my Savior is where I need to be!

Chapter 1
The Unrest

Years of turmoil and abuse will cause fear, despair, hopelessness, depression, worry, anxiety, and control. You will look at others through that wounded heart and start to believe that everyone is out to use or abuse you, including God.

God doesn't use your "wilderness period" to hurt you. The wilderness period is where you feel alone and many trials hit you. Trials will bring out into the open the negative emotions you need to get rid of along with trials to teach you. He wants to draw things out of you that are not good for your spiritual growth and to teach you who God is to you personally. After many years of a long and painful trial, this wilderness period may cause an unrest in your spirit, a spirit of restlessness and anxiety. Due to all the painful events and broken heart, it may even cause you to lose faith and not trust God. This is especially true if you suffered many years of painful events caused by others. You just want to be happy and have the hard and painful times go away fast.

The unrest or anxiety will settle into your heart and will leave you with a wrong perception of God. You have been hurt by people, and oppressed by life circumstances and bad choices. You have learned and expected that hard times and hurt caused by others is all that is in store for you. You feel as if there is no way out.

You feel as if happiness and financial freedom are not meant for you, and you have a hard time trusting that God will ever help you or set you free.

You have learned to hang on tight because letting go means trusting God, but it also means if He does not come through you will get hurt again and you cannot handle getting hurt again. So, you hang on for fear of getting hurt and try to work out your issues on your own, attempting to control everything and only trusting in yourself. This is a form of idolatry. The answer is within you, you just have not learned it yet.

"Awake, awake! Put on your strength, O Zion; Put on your beautiful garments, O Jerusalem, the holy city! For the uncircumcised and the unclean Shall no longer come to you. Shake off your dust, arise, sit down, O Jerusalem. Loose yourself from the bonds of your neck, O captive daughter of Zion!" (Isaiah 52:1–2).

When you look to the Holy Spirit within and draw upon His strength, you have the power to trust and to let go. "I can do all things through Christ who strengthens me" (Philippians 4:13). Looking to Jesus, to the Holy Spirit and making a firm decision that you are not going to roll over and play dead to the enemy's schemes to make you immobile. Get some backbone and say, "Enough is enough!" That is the meaning of Isaiah 52:1–2. Stand up in your spirit and rely on the Holy Spirit to help you rise. "If any of you lacks wisdom, let him ask of God, who gives to all liberally and without reproach, and it will be given to him" (James 1:5). Ask God to show you what you are doing wrong. Ask Him to show you what you need to do and what you need to begin declaring over yourself, your situation, your family, and your finances. "You will also declare a thing, And it will be established for you; So light will shine on your ways" (Job 22:28).

Perhaps, you are filled with frustration at where you are at in life. Maybe you have not obtained what you want out of it, you have complete unrest within. It is like a never-ending merry-go-round. You want to be free but don't know how to claim that freedom.

It is only when your frustration drives you to say, "Enough is enough," that you throw your hands up and say, "I have to trust God! I cannot take this any longer. Change has to happen!" This is when the process of change begins to happen. God cannot begin to mold you and deliver you until you give yourself and your life over to Him, placing everything in His hands. Until it is in His hands and out of yours, the freedom will not happen. Fear of being hurt will only keep you in the prison you made for yourself. The same types of things will happen over and over. Yet, God will fulfill His purpose for you; it is promised, but it cannot happen until you let Him. "Declaring the end from the beginning, And from ancient times things that are not yet done, Saying, 'My counsel shall stand, And I will do all My pleasure" (Isaiah 46:10).

Stop crying and complaining when trouble hits; it shows your lack of faith in God. Use the trouble, instead, to expect God to show up and show Himself big in your life and to bring Him glory. How can He ever show Himself to you and to mankind in big ways if there are no situations for Him to show up in? This also helps to increase your faith as well.

You cannot move forward if you are constantly looking backwards. Stop mourning over what you lost, what you did not do, or what you do not have and move forward. Be grateful for what you do have and learn to trust God, giving Him thanks for it and all the rest and He will make your deliverance happen, He will provide and He will answer your prayers. "Rejoice always, pray without ceasing, in everything give thanks; for this is the will of God in

Christ Jesus for you. Do not quench the Spirit. Do not despise prophecies. Test al things; hold fast what is good. Abstain from every form of evil. Now may the God of peace Himself sanctify you completely; and may your whole spirit, soul, and body be preserved blameless at the coming of our Lord Jesus Christ. He who calls you is faithful, who also will do it" (I Thessalonians 5:16–24).

You cannot change what is not meant for you to change. If the load is too much for you to bear, then it is not yours to bear but God's. "Blessed be the Lord, Who daily loads us with benefits, The God of our salvation! Selah" (Psalm 68:19).

When you try to carry a load not meant for you, it only succeeds in playing into the enemy's hands to steal your joy and your peace and replace it with worry, unrest, doubt, and despair. He does this enough without us helping him! Stop it! Stop fighting for the control to fix what you obviously cannot fix. God says to trust Him and cast your cares on Him. His yoke is much easier to bear when He is bearing the weight of our burdens. "Come to Me, all you who are weary and heavy laden, and I will give you rest. Take My yoke upon you and learn from Me, for I am gentle and lowly in heart, and you will find rest for your souls. For My yoke is easy and My burden is light" (Matthew 11:28–30).

Decide today to trust God, you may not be able to see ahead the path God has lined out for you, but trust in His love. He loved you enough to send Jesus to die in the place of all of mankind for our sins so He may have us with Him eternally. That is proof enough of His love, so trust Him to guide you safely through. "I will bring the blind by a way they did not know; I will lead them in paths they have not known. I will make darkness light before them, And crooked places straight. These things I will do for them, And not forsake them. They shall be turned back, They shall be greatly ashamed, Who trust in carved images, Who say to the molded images, 'You are our gods'" (Isaiah 42:16–17).

One example of determination is in the story of Jacob and Esau. In Genesis 27–33, Isaac is on his deathbed. In the Jewish custom, they used to bless the firstborn son first. Rebekah, Jacob and Esau's mother, overheard Isaac telling Esau to bring him some game that he may eat and give him his blessing. Rebekah quickly told Jacob to bring some food to his father, and pretend to be Esau. Isaac, with failing eyes and being near death, believed and blessed Jacob with the firstborn blessing. Esau became angry and Jacob fled to live for a while with his uncle Laban. Year after year went by as he worked for his uncle. He worked seven years in order to marry Rachel only to find out his uncle tricked him into marrying Leah. So he worked an additional seven years for Rachel and even longer in order to build up his flock. Jacob grew tired of being there and wanted to come home even though he was afraid of Esau. Esau threatened to kill Jacob when he took the birthright that should have been given to him. He was still determined to return. Determined, he sent gifts ahead, hoping Esau's anger would be reduced. Sometimes you must do things afraid. Courage is not the absence of fear, but is facing the issue despite being afraid of it.

Jacob had grown tired of who he was, the old self, and became determined to become the new, blessed man of God he was meant to be. You can also become who you are meant to be in Christ by throwing off the old! "But you have not so learned Christ, if indeed you have heard Him and have been taught by Him, as the truth is in Jesus: that you put off, concerning your former conduct, the old man which grows corrupt according to the deceitful lusts, and be renewed in the spirit of your mind, and that you put on the new man which was created according to God, in true righteousness and holiness" (Ephesians 4:20–24).

Stop blaming others, stop feeling sorry for yourself, stop blaming God and looking everywhere else for answers and help. Look to God!

The man at the pool of Bethesda in John 5 is an example of someone who just makes excuses. He had been there for thirty-eight years! He lay every day at the pool where an angel would stir the waters and healed those who were able to get in. Although the paralyzed man was there, he expected others to help him and his excuses kept him from his healing. How long have your excuses kept you bound? "When Jesus saw him lying there, and knew that he already had been in that condition a long time, He said to him, 'Do you want to be made well?'" (John 5:6).

He is asking you the same thing: "Do you want to be made well?"

Chapter 2
The Roadblocks

Discovering the roadblocks—the real issues—that are keeping you from letting go and trusting God is important for each step in your journey. The first step is recognizing you have a problem and having a desire to move past it. The second step is bringing God into the situation and asking for His help. "To open blind eyes, To bring out prisoners from the prison, Those who sit in darkness from the prison house" (Isaiah 42:7).

God already knows your struggle and wants you to be set free, but it will only happen when you want that same freedom. If you are not ready, you will resort back to your old habits. Instead, God waits patiently until just the right time for you to ask when you are ready. "Therefore the LORD will wait, that He may be gracious to you; And therefore He will be exalted, that He may have mercy on you. For the LORD is a God of justice; Blessed are all those who wait for Him" (Isaiah 30:18).

To discover the real issues behind your unrest, you need to discover the roadblocks that keep you from trusting God and receiving His peace. Why do you react in fear when trouble hits? Why does that fear make you angry? These negative emotions keep you bound in fear and worry, but God wants to set you free. "'For it shall come to pass in that day,' Says the LORD of hosts, 'That I will break his yoke from your neck And will burst your bonds; Foreigners shall no more enslave them'" (Jeremiah 30:8).

Anger may set in when something makes you feel guilty or full of shame. It may be brought on by a past resentment of something that happened or something that someone did causing you to be unable to let go or forgive. Sometimes anger comes from the prideful stubbornness that keeps you from forgiving. These are all roadblocks that may cause you to transfer those negative emotions on to God and keep you from trusting Him. You may trust Him in some areas, but not one hundred percent due to those issues. Instead, you worry over things that are out of your control and are not meant for you to control. Perhaps you are not able to forgive others or yourself. I say surrender! There is so much freedom in choosing to let go and so much joy and peace as well. Allow God to show you the way, to help you to forgive, to help you move past that event, and to stop being afraid. Surrender all those issues and negative emotions to God. Ask for His help. "Where do wars and fights come from among you? Do they not come from your desires for pleasure that war in your members? You lust and do not have. You murder and covet and cannot obtain. You fight and war. Yet you do not have because you do not ask. You ask and do not receive, because you ask amiss, that you may spend it on your pleasures" (James 4:1–3).

When you are anointed to do something, then it will come with ease but if you are not then it will be oppressive to you, a burden. To be anointed is like being gifted in a certain area such as preaching. Some people can preach with ease where others they would rather have their teeth pulled.

To do this you need to get alone with God and allow God to expose all. In return, tell Him all. Tell Him all your worries, fears, concerns, and the things you do not understand. He already knows, but in telling Him, you release the problem and bring it out into the light—the light of Jesus. When you release it to Him, the healing can begin. "That He would grant you, according to the riches of His glory, to be strengthened with might through His Spirit in the inner man" (Ephesians 3:16). In the Garden of Eden, Adam and Eve walked around naked—they had nothing to hide before they sinned. "But he who does the truth comes to the light, that his deeds may be clearly seen, that they have been done in God" (John 3:21).

In your alone time, God will reveal things to you and give you hope and direction. He will show you truth and expose the lies you once believed. "All things that the Father has are Mine. Therefore, I said that He will take of Mine and declare it to you" (John 16:15).

Even Jesus needed time to be alone with his Father. "When Jesus heard it, He departed from there by boat to a deserted place by Himself. But when the multitudes heard it, they followed Him on foot from the cities" (Matthew 14:13).

Discovering the truth will help you get to the root and replace the lies from Satan. "And you shall know the truth, and the truth shall make you free" (John 8:32). Learn to ask yourself why you act and react the way you do. Getting to the root will help you to discover the cause. Understanding the roadblocks in your life is one thing, but discovering why they became issues and getting past them is quite another. Finding trust will help set you free and lead you to your inner healing. God knows your heart, He created it. "But the LORD said to Samuel, 'Do not look at his appearance or at his physical stature, because I have refused him. For the LORD does not see as man sees; for man looks at the outward appearance, but the LORD looks at the heart'" (1 Samuel 16:7). God knows all the emotions within and what caused them. Trust Him to lead you safely through to victory and healing. "If we had forgotten the name of our God Or spread out our hands to a foreign god, Would not God search this out? For He knows the secrets of the heart" (Psalm 44:20–21).

Mephibosheth was dropped as a child when his nurse fled the palace. He was injured and grew up in Lo Debar, which means "pasture-less or having no place." He lived there so long, he had to be reminded he was royalty!

The pain of his injury was so great it caused him to forget and to become accustomed to Lo Debar—a hopeless existence. But God! He always has a plan. He loves us too much to let us stay in a place we were never meant to be.

Discovering the "whys" is not always an overnight process, nor is it easy, but the victory you will receive will be oh, so worth it. "Now to Him who is able to do exceedingly abundantly above all that we ask or think, according to the power that works in us" (Ephesians 3:20).

Doing things your way has not worked out too well, has it? So why do you keep insisting on trying to do everything yourself? Dare to believe and to trust God. Try something new. Doing the same thing over and over and expecting different results is sort of insane. It is like continuing to plant apple seeds and expecting an orange tree to grow—it isn't going to happen! "Trust in the LORD with all your heart, And lean not on your own understanding; In all your ways acknowledge Him, And He shall direct your paths. Do not be wise in your own eyes; Fear the LORD and turn away from evil. It will be health to your flesh, And strength to your bones" (Proverbs 3:5–8). God wants to do a new thing; will you let Him? "Do not remember the former things, Nor consider the things of old. Behold, I will do a new thing, Now it shall spring forth; shall you not know it?" (Isaiah 43:18–19).

You will never go forward if you are continually looking back at the past and what hurt you. Focusing on the past only causes you to carry it with you into the present and into the future. You allow the event to keep hurting you. You allow the person that hurt you to continue doing so even though they are gone.

Do you want to be free of worry? Do you want to be free of anger? Do you want to learn to forgive and let go once and for all? Do you want to accept God's love and forgiveness and be free of guilt and shame? "Stand fast therefore in the liberty by which Christ has made us free, and do not be entangled again with a yoke of bondage" (Galatians 5:1).

You must want freedom bad enough to move on—to get off the merry-go-round of fear, worry and despair. When you want it bad enough and made up your mind that you will be determined to stay the course no matter what, you will arrive to the place and purpose, to the victory God has for you. "Shake yourself from the dust, arise; Sit down, O Jerusalem! Loose yourself from the bonds of your neck, O captive daughter of Zion!" (Isaiah 52:2).

Jacob's name in Hebrew meant "deceiver" and he did. He deceived his brother in obtaining the inheritance meant for the oldest son and deceived his father in receiving it. To save her sons, their mother sent Jacob to live with her brother Laban. He spent years there and was deceived by Laban into marrying the older of his daughters first even though he wanted to marry the younger Rachel instead. He agreed to work an additional seven years to be able to marry Rachel, the one he really wanted to marry. Jacob worked for Laban longer than he wanted. That is what giving into the enemy's plans does—steals your joy and peace and causes you doubt God and make your own poor choices. Instead, you can choose to trust God. "I call heaven and earth as witnesses against you, that I have set before you; life and death, blessing and cursing; therefore choose life, that both you and your descendants may live; that you may love the LORD your God, that you may obey His voice, and that you may cling to Him, for He is your life, and the length of your days; and that you may dwell in the land which the Lord swore to your fathers, to

Abraham, Isaac, and Jacob, to give them" (Deuteronomy 30:19–20).

God told Jacob it was time to go home and he is telling you that now. Leave the land of fear, worry, anger, guilt, and shame. Forgive and let go. Return home to God's rest. "And He said, 'My Presence will go with you, and I will give you rest'" (Exodus 33:14). Are you tired? Do you need rest?

Jacob became tired of who he was and what he was known by, but remembered how he'd left his home and was afraid of how his brother would react when they met again. He sent his servants ahead with gifts and stayed behind and wrestled with God. He wrestled with the angel of the Lord until He blessed him. Will you hold tight to trust no matter what until you receive your victory?

"Then Jacob was left alone; and a Man wrestled with him until the breaking of day. Now when He saw that He did not prevail against him, He touched the socket of his hip; and the socket of Jacob's hip was out of joint as He wrestled with him. And He said, "Let Me go, for the day breaks." But he said, "I will not let You go unless You bless me!" So He said to him, "What is your name?" He said, "Jacob." And He said, "Your name shall no longer be called Jacob, but Israel; for you have struggled with God and with men, and have prevailed." Then Jacob asked, saying, "Tell me Your name, I pray." And He said, "Why is it that you ask about My name?" And He blessed him there. So Jacob called the name of the place Peniel: "For I have seen God face to face, and my life is preserved." Just as he crossed over Penuel the sun rose on him, and he limped on his hip. Therefore to this day the children of Israel do not eat the muscle that shrank, which is on the hip socket, because He touched the socket of Jacob's hip in the muscle that shrank (Genesis 32:24–32).

The Holy Spirit will help, and He will give you strength. All you need to do is ask. "The LORD will give strength to His people; The LORD will bless His people with peace" (Psalm 29:11).

God has good plans for you and, if you seek His plans, you will find them. It is promised!

"For I know the thoughts that I think toward you, says the Lord, thoughts of peace and not of evil, to give you a future and a hope. Then you will call upon Me and go and pray to Me, and I will listen to you. And you will seek Me and find Me, when you search for Me with all your heart. I will be found by you, says the Lord, and I will bring you back from your captivity; I will gather you from all the nations and from all the places where I have driven you, says the Lord, and I will bring you to the place from which I cause you to be carried away captive." (Jeremiah 29:11–14)

Chapter 3
Discovering the Cause

Once you have discovered the roadblocks, the next step is to discover where the pain, fear, anger, depression, and need for control came from. What or who caused you to feel or act the way you do? Many people who have suffered years of abuse may block the events as a safeguard, but that does not heal you, it only buries the pain. Those painful moments will continue to surface through your ongoing issues of fear and anger. This unhealthy way of dealing with things may lead to carnal ways—such as drug or alcohol addiction—to escape the pain. Carnal, manmade ways can never heal your heart the way our supernatural God can. He created the heart. He knows what is in your heart and what caused the pain. He is the only one who can truly heal it.

Knowing the issues are one thing, but what caused them and how you respond to those same issues can help you change your behaviors into healthier ones. Knowing what God wants for you will help you to respond in a spiritually healthy way. You can then stay in God's peace as you continue to trust in Him. This is the next step in learning to let go.

God knows your heart and He knows what has hurt you. He also knows about your dreams. "O LORD, You have searched me and known me. You know my sitting down and my rising up; You understand my thought afar off. You comprehend my path and my lying down, And are acquainted with all my ways. For there is not a word on my tongue, But behold, O LORD, You know it altogether. You have hedged me behind and before, And laid Your hand upon me. Such knowledge is too wonderful for me; It is high, I cannot attain it (Psalm 139:1–6).

God wants you whole and full of His joy and peace, but you must want to be there. When you finally grow restless and say enough is enough, determination will set in and you will finally listen to His guidance and learn from the Word of God. "when you become restless, That you shall break his yoke from your neck" (Genesis 27:40b).

Learning to ask yourself, "Why," will help you to find the reasons for your actions and negative feelings.

Every time I got scared, I would get angry. I did not realize my anger was actually fear. After I finally left my husband, it took lots of time and staying close to

God before I could reach the point when I was ready to begin asking myself the "why's."

A very dear friend, one whom I believe was a divine appointment from God, taught me this important task. She asked me, "Why? Why does that make you mad?" I asked myself that question and started searching for the answer as I prayed. God gave me the answer, the anger was rooted in fear. Every time something made me afraid—afraid of being hurt, afraid something would break my heart, afraid I would not have enough—I would get angry. It was when my friend, with wisdom given from God, helped me and opened my eyes to what my problems were and where they started from, that I could finally bring those issues to God. He wants to heal you; He wants to deliver you; but He will not force Himself on you. As He opens your eyes to the things that have you stuck, and that work to keep you from trusting Him completely, it is up to you to go to Him in prayer for help to overcome them.

It was not good enough to know I was afraid, the step that would lead to my healing was knowing *why* I was afraid. Then I could take those issues to God to find what I needed to be healed and to overcome. "And the Lord "your God will drive out those nations before you little by little; you will be unable to destroy them at once, lest the beasts of the field become too numerous for you" (Deuteronomy 7:22).

Once you know the truth behind the issue—the negative emotions or actions, the real cause—then you can go to God for the correct path to your healing. His truth will set you free. "And you shall know the truth, and the truth shall make you free" (John 8:32).

Go back to the beginning, the first time you experienced that anger or fear. Ask yourself, "What really set me off? What caused it?" If the answer related to a person that hurt you and you cannot let go of the event, or you cannot forgive them, ask yourself, "Why?" Get to the root of the issue, but do not do it alone. Ask the Holy Spirit to be with you and reveal the truth. What you cannot do in your strength, you can in His. "I can do all things through Christ who strengthens me" (Philippians 4:13).

You may be asking, why is getting to the root of my negative issues important in being able to trust God? Because the negative emotions crowd your heart much like weeds in a garden. Pull the weeds and the garden flourishes. Pull the weeds—the negative emotions—in your heart, and the fruit of the Spirit will grow. "But the fruit of the Spirit is love, joy, peace, longsuffering, kindness, goodness, faithfulness, gentleness, self-control" (Galatians 5:22–23).

Maybe the thing that keeps you stuck is your inability to let go of normal, ongoing, day-to-day issues. Issues that are not due to a person or event, but just everyday things. Or maybe your fear comes from not knowing—truly knowing—God.

In the Book of Acts 9:1-22 it tells about the conversion of Saul, who became Paul. Saul, who became Paul, is a wonderful example of not knowing the Lord. Saul had a wrong perception of God and what it meant to serve Him. That wrong perception caused him to kill Christians. He thought he was completely right in his actions. He thought those he killed were simply religious fanatics. When he was on the road to Damascus, God suddenly blinded and threw him off his horse. Saul had to be literally knocked off his high horse to have his eyes opened to the truth.

In his blind state, he saw the Lord and the Lord asked him why he was persecuting Him. In response Saul asked him, "Lord, what do you want me to do?" (Acts 9:6)

The Lord instructed him to go into the city and he would be told what to do. He was blind for three days and did not eat or drink. The men who were with him were speechless about what just happened and led him into the city. From there the Lord had visited Ananias in a vision and commanded him to go to Saul and lay hands on him and pray for him.

Ananias was hesitant but did as the Lord commanded him to do.

The Lord changed his name from Saul to Paul. Saul regained his sight and his strength and immediately began to preach.

Once his eyes were opened and he was enlightened to the truth, he became a mighty man of God. The changing of his name was a symbolism of how we are given a new life in Christ. Once our sins are forgiven, the Lord remembers our sins no more, "For I will be merciful to their unrighteousness, and their sins and their lawless deeds I will remember no more." (Hebrews 8:12)

Paul wrote thirteen of the twenty-seven books of the New Testament and five of those were from prison. All you need is a touch from God. When you start a relationship with God in faith, miracles happen. That is what happened with the woman with the issue of blood as well. She had this issue for twelve long years and tried everything, but all she had to do was touch the hem of Jesus's garment and she was healed! You can find this story in the Book of Mark 5:21-34.

Jesus said, her faith healed her. Her faith acted like a cord to a lamp. The lamp cannot light up until it connects to the power source! Faith connects! Isn't that enough to stay the course to your healing, your victory?

In the Bible there is a story about a woman named Ruth. Ruth was Naomi's daughter-in-law. Naomi learned to trust after loss of everything. She and her husband tried fix their problems on their own without asking God. Naomi learned by the trials of life as most of us do. We reach the end of our self when the trials of life wear us out and we throw our hands up in surrender, saying, "Lord, help me, please!"

Naomi and her husband Elimelech lived in Bethlehem. Bethlehem means, "Place of bread." There was a famine in the land and, instead of inquiring of the Lord, they moved without asking if it was the right thing to do. "A man's steps are of the Lord; How then can a man understand his own way?" (Proverbs 20:24)

God wants to show you the way and He says if you lack wisdom, ask. "If any of you lacks wisdom, let him ask of God, who gives to all liberally and without reproach, and it will be given to him." (James 1:5) If you are not sure, rely on Him and He will make your paths straight. "Trust in the LORD with all your heart, And lean not on your own understanding; In all your ways acknowledge Him, And He shall direct your paths." (Proverbs 3:5-6)

We will always have ups and downs in life but every time you experience rough times—a short pay week or astronomical utility bills—do you pick up and move? You never make a permanent decision in what could be temporary situation, but that is what they did. Elimelech, Naomi and their two sons picked up and moved to Moab meaning, "Who's your father." In other words, they moved from a place of bread to a place where they may have been looking at the present situation and did not remember all that their heavenly Father had done for them and brought them through in the past.

Life goes on and during the time they were in Moab their two sons married. One married Orpha and the other Ruth. Elimelech and his two sons died, and Naomi was left with her two daughters-in-law. Since she did not have any more sons for them to marry, Orpah decided to return to her homeland, but Ruth wanted to stay. "But Ruth said: 'Entreat me not to leave you, Or to turn back from following after you; For wherever you go, I will go; And wherever you lodge, I will lodge; Your people shall be my people, And your God, my God. Where you die, I will die, And there will I be buried. The LORD do so to me, and more also, If anything but death parts you and me'" (Ruth 1:16–17).

As the story continues, Ruth and Naomi return to Bethlehem and Ruth begins to glean in the fields behind the harvest workers to pick up what they left behind for herself and Naomi. Boaz—the owner of the field—noticed and was impressed by her hard work and devotion. Ruth marries Boaz and the line of Jesus is birthed. God never forgot Naomi, and he would have provided for her and her family had they stayed. Nevertheless, He will always make something good out of our mistakes. "And we know that all things work together for good to those who love God, to those who are the called according to His purpose" (Romans 8:28).

Let Ruth's story be an encouragement to you—you can trust God. Even if you make mistakes along the way, He can make something beautiful from the ashes. The line of Jesus came from Ruth and Boaz, their Kinsman-Redeemer, ours is Jesus Christ.

Chapter 4
Who Do You Say I Am?
God the Father

Getting to know who God is: He is "I AM that I AM." "And God said to Moses, "I AM WHO I AM." And He said, "Thus you shall say to the children of Israel, 'I AM has sent me to you'" (Exodus 3:14). He is the Trinity: God the Father, Jesus the Son, and the Holy Spirit. What does that mean? How does it apply to you? In this chapter and in the next two chapters, we are going to look at all three facets of the Trinity.

Whatever you need, that is who He is and so much more! To truly be able to trust Him, it helps to know who He is; Spend time with God and the Bible in order to get to know His character and His love for you. When you know that, that knowledge will help you learn to let go and trust Him, knowing that "He will not leave you or forsake you" (Deuteronomy 31:8b).

"Bless the Lord, O my soul; And all that is within me, bless His holy name!

Bless the Lord, O my soul, And forget not all His benefits: Who forgives all your iniquities, Who heals all your diseases, Who redeems your life from destruction, Who crowns you with lovingkindness and tender mercies, Who satisfies your mouth with good things, So that your youth is renewed like the eagle's. The LORD executes righteousness and justice for all who are oppressed. He made known His ways to Moses, His acts to the children of Israel. The LORD is merciful and gracious, Slow to anger, and abounding in mercy.

He will not always strive with us, Nor will He keep His anger forever. He has not dealt with us according to our sins, Nor punished us according to our iniquities. For as the heavens are high above the earth, So great is His mercy toward those who fear Him; As far as the east is from the west, So far has He removed our transgressions from us. As a father pities his children, So the Lord pities those who fear Him. For He knows our frame; He remembers that we are dust. As for man, his days are like grass; As a flower of the field, so he flourishes. For the wind passes over it, and it is gone, And its place remembers it no more. But the mercy of the LORD is from everlasting to everlasting On those who fear Him, And His righteousness to children's children, To such as keep His covenant, And to those who remember His commandments to do them. The LORD has established His throne in heaven, and His kingdom rules overall. Bless the Lord, you His angels, Who excel in strength, who do His word, Heeding the voice of His word. Bless the LORD, all you His hosts, You ministers of His, who do His pleasure. Bless the Lord, all His works, in all places of His dominion. Bless the LORD, O my soul!" (Psalm 103)

When you learn who He is and about His overwhelming love and faithfulness, then it becomes easier to let go of worry and trust Him. Who is He to you? Do you truly know Him? "He said to them, 'But who do you say that I am?' Peter answered and said to Him, 'You are the Christ'" (Mark 8:29).

Paul did not know who Jesus really was and therefore his actions followed suit. Once he was enlightened to the truth, it changed everything! "And you shall know the truth, and the truth shall make you free" (John 8:32).

That was part of my problem, I did not truly know all of whom God is to me and the extent of His love. Maybe it is part of your problem as well, As I had to, getting to know the Father, who He truly is to you and just how much He loves you will help you as it did for me. What are His character qualities? Let's take a look.

1. He has an Agape love– Agape love is an unconditional love—you do not have to earn it. God loves us first even while we sin and loves us despite ourselves. "But God demonstrates His own love toward us, in that while we were still sinners, Christ died for us" (Romans 5:8).

"We love Him because He first loved us" (I John 4:19).

"Who shall separate us from the love of Christ? Shall trouble, or distress, or persecution, or famine, or nakedness, or peril, or sword? As it is written: 'For Your sake we face death all day long; We are accounted as sheep for the slaughter.'" Yet in all these things we are more than conquerors through Him who loved us. For I am persuaded that neither death nor life, nor angels nor principalities nor powers, nor things present nor things to come, 39 nor height nor depth, nor any other created thing, shall be able to separate us from the love of God which is in Christ Jesus our Lord" (Romans 8:35–39).

"I have loved you with an everlasting love; Therefore with lovingkindness I have drawn you" (Jeremiah 31:3c).

2. He watches over you continually – "The LORD shall preserve you going out and you coming in from this time forth, and even forevermore" (Psalm 121:8).

3. He repairs and restores – "Those from among you Shall build the old waste places; You shall raise up the foundations of many generations; And you shall be called the Repairer of the Breach, The Restorer of Streets to Dwell In" (Isaiah 58:12).

4. He does not condemn – "There is therefore now no condemnation to those who are in Christ Jesus, who do not walk according to the flesh, but according to the Spirit" (Romans 8:1).

5. Always for us – "What then shall we say to these things? If God is for us, who can be against us?" (Romans 8:31).

6. He always forgives-and forgets – "For I will be merciful to their unrighteousness, and their sins and their lawless deeds I will remember no more" (Hebrews 8:12).

 "If we confess our sins, He is faithful and just and will forgive us our sins and purify us from all unrighteousness" (1 John 1:9).

7. He has mercy and compassion – "The LORD, the LORD God, the merciful and gracious, longsuffering, and abounding in goodness and truth, 7 keeping mercy for thousands, forgiving iniquity and transgression and sin, by no means clearing the guilty, visiting the iniquity of the fathers upon the children and the children's children to the third and the fourth generation" (Exodus 34:6–7).

"Therefore be merciful, just as your Father also is merciful" (Luke 6:36).

8. He Protects –" Fear not, for I have redeemed you;
I have called you by your name; You are Mine. When you pass through the waters, I will be with you; And when you pass through the rivers, they shall not overflow you. When you walk through the fire, you shall not be burned, Nor shall the flame scorch you.. For I am the LORD your God, The Holy One of Israel, your Savior" (Isaiah 43:1b–3).

"He who dwells in the secret place of the Most High Shall abide under the shadow of the Almighty. I will say of the Lord, "He is my refuge and my fortress; My God, in Him I will trust." Surely He shall deliver you from the snare of the [a]fowler
And from the perilous pestilence. He shall cover you with His feathers, And under His wings you shall take refuge; His truth shall be your shield and buckler. You shall not be afraid of the terror by night, Nor of the arrow that flies by day, Nor of the pestilence that walks in darkness, Nor of the destruction that lays waste at noonday. A thousand may fall at your side, And ten thousand at your right hand; But it shall not come near you. Only with your eyes shall you look, And see the reward of the wicked. Because you have made the Lord, who is my refuge, Even the Most High, your dwelling place,

No evil shall befall you, Nor shall any plague come near your dwelling; For He shall give His angels charge over you, To keep you in all your ways. In their hands they shall bear you up, Lest you dash your foot against a stone. You shall tread upon the lion and the cobra, The young lion and the serpent you shall trample underfoot. "Because he has set his love upon Me, therefore I will deliver him; I will [e]set him on high, because he has known My name. He shall call upon Me, and I will answer him;
I will be with him in trouble; I will deliver him and honor him. With long life I will satisfy him, And show him My salvation"." (Psalm 91).

9.   He comforts – "Yea, though I walk through the valley of the shadow of death, I will fear no evil; For You are with me; Your rod and Your staff, they comfort me" (Psalm 23:4).

10.   He guides – "He leads me in the paths of righteousness For His name's sake" (Psalm 23:3).

"You in your mercy have led forth The people whom You have redeemed; You have guided them in Your strength To Your holy habitation" (Exodus 15:13).

11.   He provides – "And my God shall supply all your need according to His riches in glory by Christ Jesus" (Philippians 4:19).

12. He disciplines as a father – "'My son, do not despise the chastening of the LORD, Nor be discouraged when you are rebuked by Him; For whom the Lord loves He chastens, And scourges every son whom He receives.' If you endure chastening, God deals with you as with sons; for what son is there whom a father does not chasten? (Hebrews 12:5–7).

"Behold, happy is the man whom God corrects; Therefore do not despise the chastening of the Almighty. For He bruises, but He binds up; He wounds, but His hands make whole'" (Job 5:17–18).

13. He hears us – "Now this is the confidence that we have in Him, that if we ask anything according to His will, He hears us" (1 John 5:14).

14. He answers us – "The eyes of the LORD are on the righteous, And His ears are open to their cry" (Psalm 34:15).

"Most assuredly, I say to you, he who believes in Me, the works that I do he will do also; and greater works than these he will do, because I go to My Father. And whatever you ask in My name, that I will do, that the Father may be glorified in the Son. If you ask anything in My name, I will do it" (John 14:12–14).

"So Jesus answered and said to them, "Have faith in God. For assuredly, I say to you, whoever says to this mountain, 'Be removed and be cast into the sea,' and does not doubt in his heart, but believes that those things he says will be done, he will have whatever he says. Therefore I say to you, whatever things you ask when you pray, believe that you receive them, and you will have them" (Mark 11:22–24)

15. He Speaks to us – "For God may speak in one way, or in another, Yet man does not perceive it" (Job 33:14).

"You go near and hear all that the LORD our God may say, and tell us all that the LORD our God says to you, and we will hear and do it" (Deuteronomy 5:27).

"But He answered and said, 'It is written, "Man shall not live by bread alone, but by every word that proceeds from the mouth of God"'" (Matthew 4:4).

16. He is our refuge – "He who dwells in the secret place of the Most High Shall abide in the shadow of the Almighty. I will say of the LORD, 'He is my refuge and my fortress; My God, in Him I will trust.' Surely He shall deliver you from the snare of the fowler And from the perilous pestilence. He shall cover you with His feathers, And under His wings you shall take refuge; His truth shall be your shield and buckler" (Psalm 91:1–4).

17. He delivers us – "The righteous cry out, and the LORD hears, And delivers them from out of their troubles. The LORD is close to those who have a broken heart, And saves such as have a contrite spirit. Many are the afflictions of the righteous, But the Lord delivers him out of them all" (Psalm 34:17–19).

18. He is faithful – "But the Lord is faithful, who will establish you and guard you from the evil one" (2 Thessalonians 3:3).

"Praise the LORD, all you Gentiles! Laud Him, all you peoples. For His merciful kindness is great toward us, And the truth of the Lord endures forever. Praise the LORD!" (Psalm 117:1–2).

"God is not a man, that He should lie, Nor a son of man, that He should repent. Has He said, and will He not do? Or has He spoken, and will He not make it good?" (Numbers 23:19).

19. He finishes what He starts in us – "Being confident of this very thing, that He who has begun a good work in you will complete it until the day of Jesus Christ" (Philippians 1:6).

20. He wants good for us – "For I know the thoughts that I think toward you, says the Lord, thoughts of peace and not of evil, to give you a future and a hope. Then you will call upon Me and go and pray to Me, and I will listen to you. And you will seek Me and find Me, when you search for Me with all your heart. I will be found by you, says the Lord, and I will bring you back from your captivity; I will gather you from all the nations and from all the places where I have driven you, says the Lord, and I will bring you to the place from which I cause you to be carried away captive" (Jeremiah 29:11–14).

21. He is patient – "The Lord is not slack concerning His promise, as some count slackness, but is longsuffering toward us, not willing that any should perish but that all should come to repentance" (2 Peter 3:9).

22. He is always with us – "O Lord, You have searched me and known me. You know my sitting down and my rising up; You understand my thought afar off. You comprehend my path and my lying down, And are acquainted with all my ways. For there is not a word on my tongue, But behold, O LORD, You know it altogether. You have hedged me behind and before, And laid Your hand upon me. Such knowledge is too wonderful for me; It is high, I cannot attain it. Where can I go from Your Spirit? Or where can I flee from Your presence? If I ascend into heaven, You are there; If I make my bed in hell, behold, You are there. If I take the wings of the morning, And dwell in the uttermost parts of the sea, Even there Your hand shall lead me, And Your right hand shall hold me. If I say, "Surely the darkness shall fall on me," Even the night shall be light about me; Indeed, the darkness shall not hide from You, But the night shines as the day; The darkness and the light are both alike to You" (Psalm 139:1–12).

23. He blesses us – "Blessed is everyone who fears the Lord, Who walks in His ways. When you eat the labor of your hands, You shall be happy, and it shall be well with you. Your wife shall be like a fruitful vine In the very heart of your house, Your children like olive plants All around your table. Behold, thus shall the man be blessed Who fears the Lord" (Psalm 128:1–4).

"Now it shall come to pass, if you diligently obey the voice of the LORD your God, to observe carefully all His commandments which I command you today, that the LORD your God will set you high above all nations of the earth. And all these blessings shall come upon you and overtake you, because you obey the voice of the LORD your God: 'Blessed shall you be in the city, and blessed shall you be in the country. Blessed shall be the [a]fruit of your body, the produce of your ground and the increase of your herds, the increase of your cattle and the offspring of your flocks. Blessed shall be your basket and your kneading bowl. Blessed shall you be when you come in, and blessed shall you be when you go out. The LORD will cause your enemies who rise against you to be defeated before your face; they shall come out against you one way and flee before you seven ways. The LORD will command the blessing on you in your storehouses and in all to which you set your hand, and He will bless you in the land which the LORD your God is giving you" (Deuteronomy 28:1–8).

24. He helps us –"God is our refuge and strength, A very present help in trouble" (Psalm 46:1).

25. He gives us grace – "But God, who is rich in mercy, because of His great love with which He loved us" (Ephesians 2:4).

26. He is gentle--"Take My yoke upon you and learn from Me, for I am gentle and lowly in heart, and you will find rest for your souls" (Matthew 11:29).

27. He gives us victory – "But thanks be to God, who gives us the victory through our Lord Jesus Christ" (1 Corinthians 15:57).

"Through God we will do valiantly, For it is He who shall tread down our enemies" (Psalm 60:12).

28. He fills us with His Holy Spirit – "Even so we, when we were children, were in bondage under the elements of the world. But when the fullness of the time had come, God sent forth His Son, born of a woman, born under the law, to redeem those who were under the law, that we might receive the adoption as sons. And because you are sons, God has sent forth the Spirit of His Son into your hearts, crying out, 'Abba, Father!' Therefore you are no longer a slave but a son, and if a son, then an heir of God through Christ" (Galatians 4:3–7).

29. He seals us – "who also has sealed us and given us the Spirit in our hearts as a guarantee" (2 Corinthians 1:22).

Once we become a child of God, we are His forever! He loved us first, all of mankind even while we are sinning against Him and calls each and every one of us. He opens our eyes to who He is and, when we accept his Son's sacrifice for us on the cross, He transforms us. He forgives our sins and forgets them—removes them as if they never existed! How many other gods can do that?

There are so many different facets of God, those are just a few. Are they enough to enlighten you to just a portion of the depths of His love? Read the Bible and you will discover His love and mercy. He is always waiting and willing to forgive, deliver, heal, renew, and restore. Once you understand that and learn to let go of the worry and anger, it will be a lot easier to trust Him and give Him complete control of your life. Read the Word of God; it is alive and active.

"For the word of God is living and powerful, and sharper than any two-edged sword, piercing even to the division of soul and spirit, and of joints and marrow, and is a discerner of the thoughts and intents of the heart" (Hebrews 4:12).

As you read the verses that you really need your heart to receive and understand, speak them out loud. When your heart hears, faith grows.

"So then faith comes by hearing, and hearing by the word of God" (Romans 10:17).

Nothing else can fill us the way God does, love us the way He loves us, or save us they way He saves. No one here on earth would sacrifice for you the way Christ did. No one can truly comprehend the vastness of His love. As you grasp even just a little, it will help you to let go and trust Him. Here are just a few of His many names:

Jehovah--Self-existent, I Am that I Am-whatever we need is who He is.
Elohim--Strong one -He is all powerful. No one or nothing is mightier!
Adonai-Lord- He is God, Lord He should be Lord

over everything
El Elyon--Most High God
El Olam--Everlasting God
El Shaddai--Almighty God
El Roi--The Strong One
Yahweh--I am the One; Isarael's Covenant God
Jehovah Jireh--The Lord Provides
Jehovah Nissi--The Lord is my Banner
Jehovah Shalom--The Lord is Peace
Jehovah Raah/Rohi--The Lord is my Shepherd
Jehovah Rophe--The Lord Heals
Jehovah Shammah--The Lord who is Present
Jehovah Tsidkenu--The Lord our Righteousness
Jehovah Mekadesh--The Lord your Sanctifier
Jehovah Sabbaoth--The Lord of Hosts
Jehovah El Gmolah--The Lord God of Recompense
Jehovah Nakeh--The Lord who Smites
Jehovah Ezer--The Lord our Helper

Our God is Omniscient, Omnipresent, and Omnipotent—all-knowing, all present, and all-powerful. Is He your God? After reading this chapter about His love for you, doesn't that make you want to remedy the lack of Him in your heart? Most of all, read the best love story ever written: the Bible.

I pray for each and everyone of you:

"that Christ may dwell in your hearts through faith;

that you, being rooted and grounded in love, may be able to comprehend with all the saints what is the width and length and depth and height—to know the love of Christ which passes knowledge; that you may be filled with all the fullness of God." (Ephesians 3:17–19)

Chapter 5
Jesus the Son

Jesus is the way; "Jesus said to him, 'I am the way, the truth, and the life. No one comes to the Father except through Me.'" (John 14:6) He is the reason we can receive eternal Life. "Inasmuch then as the children have partaken of flesh and blood, He Himself likewise shared in the same, that through death He might destroy him who had the power of death, that is, the devil, and release those who through fear of death were all their lifetime subject to bondage. For indeed He does not give aid to angels, but He does give aid to the seed of Abraham. Therefore, in all things He had to be made like His brethren, that He might be a merciful and faithful High Priest in things pertaining to God, to make propitiation for the sins of the people. For in that He Himself has suffered, being tempted, He is able to aid those who are tempted" (Hebrews 2:14–18).

He left His home in heaven to become man, flesh, sin. He is the written Word, the spoken Word, and the living Word. "In the beginning was the Word, and the Word was with God, and the Word was

God. He was in the beginning with God" (John 1:1–2).

"The Word became flesh and dwelt among us" (John 1:14).

The world was formless and void before God spoke it into being. "In the beginning God created the heavens and the earth. The earth was without form, and void; and darkness was on the face of the deep. And the Spirit of God was hovering over the face of the waters. Then God said, 'Let there be light'; and there was light. And God saw the light, that it was good; and God divided the light from the darkness" (Genesis 1:1–4).

Jesus is the light of the world; "Then Jesus spoke to them again, saying, 'I am the light of the world. He who follows Me shall not walk in darkness, but have the light of life'" (John 8:12). Whenever you are going through a troubled time, when there is something you just cannot see clear to maneuver through, ask Jesus and He will illuminate your path.

Through Jesus and His Holy Spirit, He restores joy, it is Satan who steals it. "The thief does not come except to steal, and to kill, and to destroy. I have come that they may have life, and that they may have it more abundantly" (John 10:10).

1. He became sin for us--"My little children, these

things I write to you, so that you may not sin. And if anyone sins, we have an Advocate with the Father, Jesus Christ the righteous. And He Himself is the propitiation for our sins, and not for ours only but also for the whole world" (1 John 2:1–2)

"But He was wounded for our transgressions, He was bruised for our iniquities; The chastisement for our peace was upon Him, And by His stripes we are healed. All we like sheep have gone astray; We have turned, everyone, to his own way; And the Lord has laid on Him the iniquity of us all" (Isaiah 53:5–6).

"As you therefore have received Christ Jesus the Lord, so walk in Him, rooted and built up in Him and established in the faith, as you have been taught, abounding in it with thanksgiving. Beware lest anyone cheat you through philosophy and empty deceit, according to the tradition of men, according to the basic principles of the world, and not according to Christ. For in Him dwells all the fullness of the Godhead bodily; and you are complete in Him, who is the head of all principality and power. In Him you were also circumcised with the circumcision made without hands, by putting off the body of the sins of the flesh, by the circumcision of Christ, buried with Him in baptism, in which you also were raised with Him through faith in the working of God, who raised Him from the dead. And you, being dead in your trespasses and the uncircumcision of your flesh, He has made alive together with Him, having forgiven you all trespasses, having wiped out the handwriting of requirements that was against us, which was contrary to us. And He has taken it out of the way, having nailed it to the cross. Having disarmed principalities and powers, He made a public spectacle of them, triumphing over them in it" (Colossians 2:6–15).

2. He died for us— "For God so loved the world that He gave His only begotten Son, that whoever believes in Him should not perish but have everlasting life" (John 3:16).
"Greater love has no one than this, than to lay down one's life for his friends" (John 15:13).
By His death and resurrection, when we believe and receive, the blood of His sacrifices saves us from our sin, and we receive everlasting life. "But as many as received Him, to them He gave the right to become children of God, to those who believe in His name" (John 1:12).

3. He saves us--"But God, who is rich in mercy, because of His great love with which He loved us, even when we were dead in trespasses, made us alive together with Christ (by grace you have been saved), and raised us up together, and made us sit together in the heavenly places in Christ Jesus, that in the ages to come He might show the exceeding riches of His grace in His kindness toward us in Christ Jesus. For by grace you have been saved through faith, and that not of yourselves; it is the gift of God, not of

works, lest anyone should boast. For we are His workmanship, created in Christ Jesus for good works, which God prepared beforehand that we should walk in them" (Ephesians 2:4–10).
"Nor is there salvation in any other, for there is no other name under heaven given among men by which we must be saved" (Acts 4:12).

And because of that we are free from sin, our sin is nailed to the cross.

4. He sets us free from sins— "In Him we have redemption through His blood, the forgiveness of sins, according to the riches of His grace which He made to abound toward us in all wisdom and prudence" (Ephesians 1:7-8).

5. He gives us eternal life—" And we know that the Son of God has come and has given us understanding, that we may know Him who is true; and we are in Him who is true, in His Son Jesus Christ. This is the true God and eternal life" (1 John 5:20).

6. He intercedes— "Therefore He is also able to save to the uttermost those who come to God through Him, since He always lives to make intercession for them" (Hebrews 7:25). or 5:21

7. He sanctifies us--"Sanctify them by Your truth. Your word is truth. As You sent Me into the world, I also have sent them into the world. And for their sakes I sanctify Myself, that they also may be sanctified by the truth" (John 17:17–19).

8. He makes us righteous-- "For He made Him who knew no sin to be sin for us, that we might become the righteousness of God in Him" (2 Corinthians 5:21).

9. He purifies us--"But if we walk in the light as He is in the light, we have fellowship with one another, and the blood of Jesus His Son cleanses us from all sin" (I John 1:7).

10. We have a path to God through His death— "For through Him we both have access by one Spirit to the Father" (Ephesians 2:18).
"Therefore, having been justified by faith, we have peace with God through our Lord Jesus Christ, through whom also we have access by faith into this grace in which we stand, and rejoice in hope of the glory of God" (Romans 5:1–2).
"I am the door. If anyone enters by Me, he will be saved, and will go in and out and find pasture" (John 10:9).

11. He gives us strength— "My flesh and my heart may fail; But God is the strength of my heart and my portion forever" (Psalm 73:26).
"I can do all things through Christ who strengthens me" (Philippians 4:13).

12. He heals— "And Peter said to him, 'Aeneas, Jesus the Christ heals you. Arise and make your bed.' Then he arose immediately" (Acts 9:34).
"For He healed many, so that as many as had afflictions pressed about Him to touch Him" (Mark 3:10).
"Then the blind and the lame came to Him in the temple, and He healed them" (Matthew 21:14).

13. He delivers and sets free— "How God anointed Jesus of Nazareth with the Holy Spirit and with power, who went about doing good and healing all who were oppressed by the devil, for God was with Him" (Acts 10:38).
"As well as those who were tormented with unclean spirits. And they were healed" (Luke 6:18).

14. God's grace is through His death--"In Him we have redemption through His blood, the forgiveness of sins, according to the riches of His grace which He made to abound toward us in all wisdom and prudence" (Ephesians 1:7–8).

15. He gives us faith—"Therefore we also, since we are surrounded by so great a cloud of witnesses, let us lay aside every weight, and the sin which so easily ensnares us, and let us run with endurance the race that is set before us, looking unto Jesus, the author and finisher of our faith, who for the joy that was set before Him endured the cross, despising the shame, and has sat down at the right hand of the throne of God." (Hebrews 12:1-2).

16. He makes us holy— "By that will we have been sanctified through the offering of the body of Jesus Christ once for all" (Hebrews 10:10).

17. Makes our path straight--"Every valley shall be filled And every mountain and hill brought low; The crooked places shall be made straight and the rough ways smooth" (Luke 3:5).

18. Makes us New! – "Therefore, if anyone is in Christ, he is a new creation; old things have passed away; behold, all things have become new" (2 Corinthians 5:17).

Do you want your joy back? Do you want to get rid of all your anxiety? Do you want to stop worrying about too many bills and not enough money, that wayward child, a job loss, or a major illness? Do you want to learn to forgive and let go of the anger? Then truly look into all the Jesus is and invite Him into your life if you have not already. Ask Him to open your eyes to see, your ears to hear, and your heart to understand. Getting to know Him is an important step in letting go and trusting God completely.

Just believe, repent, ask, and receive—it is that easy.

"That if you confess with your mouth the Lord

Jesus and believe in your heart that God has raised Him from the dead, you will be saved. For with the heart one believes unto righteousness, and with the mouth confession is made unto salvation (Romans 10:9–10).

"But as many as received Him, to them He gave the right to become children of God, to those who believe in His name" (John 1:12).

Chapter 6
The Holy Spirit

The Holy Spirit comes to indwell in our hearts as the result of the death and resurrection of Jesus Christ upon us asking Him into our hearts through faith.

"But this He spoke concerning the Spirit, whom those believing in Him would receive; for the Holy Spirit was not yet *given,* because Jesus was not yet glorified" (John 7:39).

"Now hope does not disappoint, because the love of God has been poured out in our hearts by the Holy Spirit who was given to us" (Romans 5:5).

The Holy Spirit immediately comes to live within our hearts. We receive the Fruit of His Spirit as well.

Fruit of the Spirit--"But the fruit of the Spirit is love, joy, peace, longsuffering, kindness, goodness, faithfulness, gentleness, self-control" (Galatians 5:22–23).

The Holy Spirit helps us to do what we cannot. Jesus Christ came as man and was fully God and fully man. "For in Him dwells all the fullness of the Godhead bodily; and you are complete in Him, who is the head of all principality and power" (Colossians 2:9–10).

Because of this, the Holy Spirit Convicts—He convicts us and lets us know when we are doing wrong, we sense it. When we are doing right, we feel that by the peace we feel in our hearts. "And when He has come, He will convict the world of sin, and of righteousness, and of judgment" (John 16:8).

We are not suddenly a perfect person—we must grow spiritually. Our hearts are made new through the indwelling of the Holy Spirit, but we have years of the world in our minds. To fix that, our minds need to be renewed. This is done day by day, walking in the Spirit, obeying God, and spending time with Him and reading the Word.

"All Scripture is given by inspiration of God, and is profitable for doctrine, for reproof, for correction, for instruction in righteousness, that the man of God may be complete, thoroughly equipped for every good work" (2 Timothy 3:16–17).

"I beseech you therefore, brethren, by the mercies of God, that you present your bodies a living sacrifice, holy, acceptable to God, which is your reasonable service. And do not be conformed to this world, but be transformed by the renewing of your mind, that you may prove what is that good and acceptable and perfect will of God" (Romans 12:1–2).

Trials will transform us as well because most of us learn by experience. Trials will teach us, draw something out of us, correct us, and make us aware of sin in our life. "My brethren, count it all joy when you fall into various trials, knowing that the testing of your faith produces patience. But let patience have its perfect work, that you may be perfect and complete, lacking nothing" (James 1:2–4).

"Blessed be the God and Father of our Lord Jesus Christ, who according to His abundant mercy has begotten us again to a living hope through the resurrection of Jesus Christ from the dead, to an inheritance incorruptible and undefiled and that does not fade away, reserved in heaven for you, who are kept by the power of God through faith for salvation ready to be revealed in the last time. In this you greatly rejoice, though now for a little while, if need be, you have been grieved by various trials, that the genuineness of your faith, being much more precious than gold that perishes, though it is tested by fire, may be found to praise, honor, and glory at the revelation of Jesus Christ, whom having not seen you love. Though now you do not see Him, yet believing, you rejoice with joy inexpressible and full of glory, receiving the end of your faith—the salvation of your souls" (1 Peter 1:3–9).

As we continue our walk with the Lord, allowing Him to prune us, we will grow spiritually. "But He answered and said, 'Every plant, which My heavenly Father has not planted will be uprooted" (Matthew 15:13).

"Therefore, having been justified by faith, we have peace with God through our Lord Jesus Christ, through whom also we have access by faith into this grace in which we stand, and rejoice in hope of the glory of God. And not only that, but we also glory in tribulations, knowing that tribulation produces perseverance; and perseverance, character; and character, hope. Now hope does not disappoint, because the love of God has been poured out in our hearts by the Holy Spirit who was given to us" (Romans 5:1–5).

Besides aiding us in our spiritual growth, the Holy Spirit helps us in our everyday life. As you learn that He is your friend, and is for you, your trust in God will grow and become stronger and stronger. "A man who has friends must himself be friendly, But there is a friend who sticks closer than a brother" (Proverbs 18:24).

"But we all, with unveiled face, beholding as in a mirror the glory of the Lord, are being transformed into the same image from glory to glory, just as by the Spirit of the Lord" (2 Corinthians 3:18).

In our daily walk, learning to be the hands, the feet, the voice, and the heart of God to a world that is lost, the Holy Spirit becomes so much more to us. He empowers us to live in and be the image and representative of God. He helps us to be Christ's ambassadors. An ambassador represents a country and, as Christ's, we represent Him. "Now then, we are ambassadors for Christ, as though God were pleading through us: we implore you on Christ's behalf, be reconciled to God" (2 Corinthians 5:20).

Here are a few ways in which we are helped and empowered by the Holy Spirt to walk in the Spirit. "I say then: Walk in the Spirit, and you shall not fulfill the lust of the flesh" (Galatians 5:16). As we walk in the Spirit, His living water, all of who He is will flow from within. "He who believes in Me, as the Scripture has said, out of his heart will flow rivers of living water" (John 7:38).

1. Comforter— "But when the Helper comes, whom I shall send to you from the Father, the Spirit of truth who proceeds from the Father, He will testify of Me" (John 15:26).

2. Guides us into truth, speaks to us—tells us what Father says— "However, when He, the Spirit of truth, has come, He will guide you into all truth;

for He will not speak on His own authority, but whatever He hears He will speak; and He will tell you things to come" (John 16:13).

3. Power of God— "And He said to them, 'Go into all the world and preach the gospel to every creature. He who believes and is baptized will be saved; but he who does not believe will be condemned. And these signs will follow those who believe: In My name they will cast out demons; they will speak with new tongues; they will take up serpents; and if they drink anything deadly, it will by no means hurt them; they will lay hands on the sick, and they will recover'" (Mark 16:15–18).

"Then the Spirit of the LORD will come upon you, and you will prophesy with them and be turned into another man" (1 Samuel 10:6).

"But you will receive power when the Holy Spirit comes on you" (Acts 1:8a).

"For God has not given us a spirit of fear, but of power and of love and of a sound mind" (2 Timothy 1:7).

"I indeed baptize you with water unto repentance, but He who is coming after me is mightier than I, whose sandals I am not worthy to carry. He will baptize you with the Holy Spirit and fire" (Matthew 3:11).

4. Counselor— "And I will pray the Father, and He will give you another Helper, that He may abide with you forever—the Spirit of truth" (John 14:16–17a).

5. Makes intercession for us— "Likewise the Spirit also helps in our weaknesses. For we do not know what we should pray for as we ought, but the Spirit Himself makes intercession for us with groanings which cannot be uttered. Now He who searches the hearts knows what the mind of the Spirit is, because He makes intercession for the saints according to the will of God" (Romans 8:26–27).

6. Gifts of the Spirit-- The gifts of the Spirit are broken down into three basic groups, which are: Domata Gifts (equipping the Church or ministries), Charismata Gifts (stewardship gifts or ability gifts), and Pneumatic Charismata Gifts (spiritual gifts for dynamic manifestations of the Holy Spirit in which He openly displays Himself). There are three categories within the Pneumatic Charismata Gifts found in 1 Corinthians 12, which are the major gifts: Revelation Gifts, Vocal Gifts, and Power Gifts.

You need faith and the willingness to surrender to the Holy Spirit to operate in these gifts from Him. You need to be able to surrender without fear or doubt and, when He does work through you in one of these gifts, trust that it is from and through Him.

Satan will not do anything that will benefit, heal, or edify someone. He only comes to destroy. The Revelation Gifts are: Word of Wisdom, Word of Knowledge, and Discerning of Spirits. The Vocal Gifts are speaking in tongues, interpretation of tongues, and gifts of prophecy. (Dreams and visions fall into this category and are found in Acts 2:17–18).

If someone who speaks in tongues an interpreter must be present. Speaking in tongues is done to edify or build up the church. "I wish you all spoke with tongues, but even more that you prophesied; for he who prophesies is greater than he who speaks with tongues, unless indeed he interprets, that the church may receive edification" (1 Corinthians 14:5)." If one speaks in tongues in private to himself as in praying to or praising God, it builds up his faith. "He who speaks in a tongue edifies himself, but he who prophesies edifies the church" (1 Corinthians 14:4). This gives you a greater awareness that you are filled with the Holy Spirit, which increases your faith in knowing that God is with you and loves you.

The Power Gifts are faith, healing, and miracles.

It does not matter what gift you have; each one is needed and important. In Christ, we are all the "body of Christ" and each part is needed to make it complete. "For as the body is one and has many members, but all the members of that one body, being many, are one body, so also is Christ. For by one Spirit we were all baptized into one body—whether Jews or Greeks, whether slaves or free—and have all been made to drink into one Spirit" (1 Corinthians 12:12–13)."

God gives us the spiritual gifts that best fits us, and we are all to work together for the good of all people and for the unity of the whole body of Christ. "But our presentable parts have no need. But God composed the body, having given greater honor to that part which lacks it, that there should be no [h]schism in the body, but that the members should have the same care for one another. And if one member suffers, all the members suffer with it; or if one member is honored, all the members rejoice with it" (1 Corinthians 12:24–26)."

The different spiritual gifts or callings given by the Lord are found in the book of Acts, Romans, 1 Corinthians, and Ephesians. In Romans 12 and 1 Corinthians 12, the Scriptures list the Charismata Gifts, or stewardship gifts, such as teaching, serving, giving (being generous), encouragement, and leadership. It also instructs us to be hospitable. These verses also list the gifts of administration and of helping others. The gifts listed in the book of Ephesians are the Domata Gifts, or Gifts of Office, which apply to evangelists, pastors, and apostles.

"Now concerning spiritual gifts, brethren, I do not want you to be ignorant: You know that you were Gentiles, carried away to these dumb idols, however you were led. Therefore I make known to you that no one speaking by the Spirit of God calls Jesus accursed, and no one can say that Jesus is Lord except by the Holy Spirit. There are diversities of gifts, but the same Spirit. There are differences of ministries, but the same Lord. And there are diversities of activities, but it is the same God who works all in all. But the manifestation of the Spirit is given to each one for the profit of all: for to one is given the word of wisdom through the Spirit, to another the word of knowledge through the same Spirit, to another faith by the same Spirit, to another gifts of healings by the same Spirit, to another the working of miracles, to another prophecy, to another discerning of spirits, to another different kinds of tongues, to another the interpretation of tongues. But one and the same Spirit works all these things, distributing to each one individually as He wills"" (1 Corinthians 12:1–11).

Learning to trust the Holy Spirit, to know He is your friend, is imperative in learning to surrender all. He is the closest friend you will ever have. Learning to let go of worry and control gives the reins of your life over to Him. Once you learn to do this, the freedom you will feel will be overwhelming. You will ask yourself, "Why didn't I do this sooner?"

"Stand fast therefore in the liberty by which Christ has made us free, and do not be entangled again with a yoke of bondage" (Galatians 5:1).

"I have been crucified with Christ; it is no longer I who live, but Christ lives in me; and the life which I now live in the flesh I live by faith in the Son of God, who loved me and gave Himself for me" (Galatians 2:20).

You will experience overwhelming freedom and will find true rest for your soul.

"Come to Me, all you who labor and are heavy laden, and I will give you rest" (Matthew 11:28).

Chapter 7
Discovering Your Identity

Once you know who God is then you will be able to discover who you are in Christ. Knowing who you are in Christ gives you great strength and helps you to continue to believe in His love. You have to know Him fully in order to know who you are. When you truly understand that, when you understand the fact that you are an heir of Christ, it is a mighty revelation! "The Spirit Himself bears witness with our spirit that we are children of God, and if children, then heirs—heirs of God and joint heirs with Christ, if indeed we suffer with Him, that we may also be glorified together"" (Romans 8:16–17).

Being confident in Him and His love for you gives you strength, faith, courage, and fortitude to stand firm through any difficulty or trial. You will no longer worry or give way to fear. Knowing God helps you to live in His freedom! "Therefore if the Son makes you free, you shall be free indeed"" (John 8:36).

You are so important to God that even something as small as the hairs on our head are numbered! (Matthew 10:30). Believe in who you are in Christ!

It does not matter what you have done that determines God's love for you. He loves us with an agape love that is an unconditional love. He loved us first while sinning against Him and He still chose to die for us. That is love. "But God demonstrates His own love toward us, in that while we were still sinners, Christ died for us" (Romans 5:8).

What determines who you are in Christ is not what you have done now or in the past, but in your confession.

"But as many as received Him, to them He gave the right to become children of God, to those who believe in His name" (John 1:12).

"But what does it say? 'The word is near you, in your mouth and in your heart' (that is, the word of faith which we preach): that if you confess with your mouth the Lord Jesus and believe in your heart that God has raised Him from the dead, you will be saved. For with the heart one believes unto righteousness, and with the mouth confession is made unto salvation" (Romans 10:8–10).

"For by grace you have been saved through faith, and that not of yourselves; it is the gift of God, not of works, lest anyone should boast. For we are His workmanship, created in Christ Jesus for good works, which God prepared beforehand that we should walk in them" (Ephesians 2:8–10).

God will allow your world to be shaken out of your control so you will finally throw up your hands in surrender and discover who He is by trusting Him. So, you will finally discover who you are in Christ and just how precious and loved you are by Him. You are His child!

"Is He not your Father, who bought you? Has He not made you and established you? 'Remember the days of old, Consider the years of many generations. Ask your father, and he will show you; Your elders, and they will tell you: When the Most High divided their inheritance to the nations, When He separated the sons of Adam, He set the boundaries of the peoples. According to the number of the children of Israel. For the LORD's portion is His people; Jacob is the place of His inheritance. He found him in a desert land And in the wasteland, a howling wilderness; He encircled him, He instructed him, He kept him as the apple of His eye. As an eagle stirs up its nest, Hovers over its young, spreading out its wings, taking them up, Carrying them on its wings, So the LORD alone led him, And there was no foreign god with him. He made him ride in the heights of the earth, That he might eat the produce of the fields'" (Deuteronomy 32:6b–13a).

God will use the trials that come your way as a way of shaking the negative off of you. Shaking that negativity off will remove the weak things like worry, doubt, fear, shame, guilt, self-pity, and self-preservation so the strong things of God remain. "'Yet once more I shake not only the earth, but also heaven.'" Now this, 'Yet once more,' indicates the removal of those things that are being shaken, as of things that are made, that the things which cannot be shaken may remain. Therefore, since we are receiving a kingdom which cannot be shaken, let us have grace, by which we may serve God acceptably with reverence and godly fear. For our God is a consuming fire" (Hebrews 12:26–29).

When you let go of the past and the people that hurt you, the wrong that you did and God forgave you of, and the anger, shame, and guilt you will begin to grow. Letting go is choosing to trust that God has you and will not allow you to fall. "Cast your burden on the Lord, And He shall sustain you; He shall never permit the righteous to be moved." (Psalm 55:22) Letting go is deciding to forgive and place all those that hurt you in His hands to take care of; "Repay no one evil for evil. Have regard for good things in the sight of all men. If it is possible, as much as depends on you, live peaceably with all men. Beloved, do not avenge yourselves, but *rather* give place to wrath; for it is written, "Vengeance *is* Mine, I will repay," says the Lord (Romans 12:17-19)

Letting go is choosing to believe in who He says you are; a child of the Most High God. Let go and begin to believe in who you are in Christ and walk in the spirit.

"I say then: Walk in the Spirit, and you shall not fulfill the lust of the flesh. For the flesh lusts against the Spirit, and the Spirit against the flesh; and these are contrary to one another, so that you do not do the things that you wish. But if you are led by the Spirit, you are not under the law. Now the works of the flesh are evident, which are: adultery, fornication, uncleanness, lewdness, idolatry, sorcery, hatred, contentions, jealousies, outbursts of wrath, selfish ambitions, dissensions, heresies, envy, murders, drunkenness, revelries, and the like; of which I tell you beforehand, just as I also told you in time past, that those who practice such things will not inherit the kingdom of God. But the fruit of the Spirit is love, joy, peace, longsuffering, kindness, goodness, faithfulness, gentleness, self-control. Against such there is no law. And those who are Christ's have crucified the flesh with its passions and desires. If we live in the Spirit, let us also walk in the Spirit. Let us not become conceited, provoking one another, envying one another" (Galatians 5:16–26).

As you walk in the Spirit, the Fruit of the Holy Spirit that helps you to be strong will grow. The strong fruit from God are faith, hope, love, and perseverance.

"Therefore, having been justified by faith, we have peace with God through our Lord Jesus Christ, through whom also we have access by faith into this grace in which we stand, and rejoice in hope of the glory of God. And not only that, but we also glory in tribulations, knowing that tribulation produces perseverance; and perseverance, character; and character, hope. Now hope does not disappoint, because the love of God has been poured out in our hearts by the Holy Spirit who was given to us" (Romans 5:1–5).

"Blessed be the God and Father of our Lord Jesus Christ, who according to His abundant mercy has begotten us again to a living hope through the resurrection of Jesus Christ from the dead, to an inheritance incorruptible and undefiled and that does not fade away, reserved in heaven for you, who are kept by the power of God through faith for salvation ready to be revealed in the last time. In this you greatly rejoice, though now for a little while, if need be, you have been grieved by various trials, that the genuineness of your faith, being much more precious than gold that perishes, though it is tested by fire, may be found to praise, honor, and glory at the revelation of Jesus Christ, whom having not seen you love. Though now you do not see Him, yet believing, you rejoice with joy inexpressible and full of glory, receiving the end of your faith—the salvation of your souls" (1 Peter 1:3–9).

When you grow in your relationship in Christ, when you grow spiritually, you will begin to realize who you are in Him. You grow by:

1. Spending time with Him daily.
2. Reading the Bible.
3. Praying and talking. (Not simply asking for things. He is your Father and delights to hear from you besides your "911" list of needs).
4. Praising Him. (No one likes to have someone come to them just to ask for things.)
5. Obeying Him.
6. Serving. Learn to put others first as He tells us to in His Word. This is a sign of unselfishness. Afterall, He did that for us.
7. Allowing Him to teach you.
8. Repenting of your sins when He convicts you.
9. Showing humility
10.   Going to church and fellowshipping with other believers.

All these things will help you to grow spiritually and grow closer to Him. As you grow day by day your confidence in who you are will soar!

Esther, you may know her story. She was orphaned and her older cousin Mordecai adopted her and brought her up as his own daughter. They were taken when Jerusalem was taken captive. "In Shushan the citadel there was a certain Jew whose name was Mordecai the son of Jair, the son of

Shimei, the son of Kish, a Benjamite. Kish had been carried away from Jerusalem with the captives who had been captured with Jeconiah king of Judah, whom Nebuchadnezzar the king of Babylon had carried away. And Mordecai had brought up Hadassah, that is, Esther, his uncle's daughter, for she had neither father nor mother. The young woman was lovely and beautiful. When her father and mother died, Mordecai took her as his own daughter" (Esther 2:5–7). In the province they were in, it was under the kingdom of King Ahasuerus. His wife, Queen Vashti, had angered him, and his advisors suggested he bring in someone else to take over as queen, someone that respected him.

Esther and many other women were taken from their families and, after twelve months of prepping, shown to the king. Esther won the king's favor over every girl that was taken to the palace. She became queen. At first, she did not reveal her Jewish identity, but a time was coming when it would be necessary. There was trouble coming at the hand of Haman who served high in the king's palace. Haman did not like the Jews and he wanted them dead. Mordecai learned of the plot and warned Esther. At first, she was hesitant to speak to the king about this plot because no one went to the king unless summoned, even the queen. "Then Esther spoke to Hathach, and gave him a command for Mordecai: 'All the king's servants and the people of the king's provinces know that any man or woman who goes into the inner court to the king, who has not been called, he has but one law: put all to death, except the one to whom the king holds out the golden scepter, that he may live. Yet I myself have not been called to go into the king these thirty days.' So, they told Mordecai Esther's words" (Esther 4:10–12).

She called for a fast among the Jewish people. After the fast was complete, she went before the king. It was only in knowing who she truly was, a daughter of the Most High God, that she could go before the king in courage. You may face some very traumatic and very scary situations in life just like Esther. You must always remember who you are and who you belong to! You are a child of the King of Kings!

She went before the king and, due to her favor, the king permitted her to speak. She told him she wanted to have a banquet and invite Haman. The night of the banquet she told the king of his plot to kill her people. God had prepared the king's heart even before the banquet. He inspired the king to look back through the chronicles where important things were recorded. The king discovered it was Mordecai who had warned of a plot to kill the king. The king also discovered that Mordecai, a Jew, had never been recognized for his heroic act to protect the king. This would help the king to have mercy on the Jews. The king had Haman killed.

God had Esther's back and will always have yours and mine as well. Never doubt His overwhelming love for you. Even when you sin, He still loves you and still sees the sinless blood of Jesus covering you and calls you His child. Knowing His overwhelming love for you and knowing who you are will not only help you to let go and give the reins over to Him but will also help you to ask for forgiveness when needed. You will be confident you can go to the Lord and repent, knowing He will still love you and will still forgive you. "But if we walk in the light as He is in the light, we have fellowship with one another, and the blood of Jesus Christ His Son cleanses us from all sin. If we say that we have no sin, we deceive ourselves, and the truth is not in us. If we confess our sins, He is faithful and just to forgive us our sins and to cleanse us from all unrighteousness" (I John 1:7–9).

Saul was the first king but did not obey what Samuel the prophet commanded him. Instead of owning up to his disobedience, he tried to justify it. His pride showed through and the Lord decided his kingdom would be taken from him. "But now your kingdom shall not continue. The Lord has sought for Himself a man after His own heart, and the Lord has commanded him to be commander over His people, because you have not kept what the Lord commanded you" (I Samuel 13:14). He raised up David to take his place. "And when He had removed him, He raised up for them David as king, to whom also He gave testimony and said, 'I have found David the son of Jesse, a man after My own heart, who will do all My will'" (Acts 13:22).

This is not because David was perfect—he was far from it, just like you and me. David continually sought God, however, and knew he was a child of God. Even as a boy, he had a humble heart. King David is a great example of knowing who you are as a child of God. When David became king he sinned and when he became aware of his sins, he humbled himself, accepted his sin and correction, repented, and moved on. He did not allow his sins to stop him from following God, he continued regardless.

David committed adultery and had the woman's husband he was involved with sent to the front lines in battle. The man was killed and David knew this; and yet God still called him, "a man after my own heart." David repented of his sin and still continued to follow the Lord.

Do not get scared while still on the path. You can make it! You can do anything through Jesus Christ. "Rejoice in the Lord always. Again, I will say, rejoice! Let your gentleness be known to all men. The Lord is at hand. Be anxious for nothing, but in everything by prayer and supplication, with thanksgiving, let your requests be made known to God; and the peace of God, which surpasses all understanding, will guard your hearts and minds through Christ Jesus. Finally, brethren, whatever things are true, whatever things are noble, whatever things are just, whatever things are pure, whatever things are lovely, whatever things are of good report, if there is any virtue and if there is anything praiseworthy—meditate on these things. The things which you learned and received and heard and saw in me, these do, and the God of peace will be with you. But I rejoiced in the Lord greatly that now at last your care for me has flourished again; though you surely did care, but you lacked opportunity. Not that I speak in regard to need, for I have learned in whatever state I am, to be content: I know how to be abased, and I know how to abound. Everywhere and in all things, I have learned both to be full and to be hungry, both to abound and to suffer need. I can do all things through Christ who strengthens me" (Philippians 4:4–13).

During the shaking process, the trials that God allows to weed out the impurities within your heart, do not try to hang on to the fruitless and dead things out of comfort. When God begins to shake things off, stay close to Him and ask for strength, He will give it and through His Holy Spirit. He will help you to endure and provide and protect you along the way. "You lust and do not have. You murder and covet and cannot obtain. You fight and war. Yet you do not have because you do not ask" (James 4:2).

You are royalty, a royal priesthood, princes and

princesses in Christ, His heir.

"The royal daughter is all glorious within the palace; Her clothing is woven with gold" (Psalm 45:13).

"And if you are Christ's, then you are Abraham's seed, and heirs according to the promise" (Galatians 3:29).

"Therefore you are no longer a slave but a son, and if a son, then an heir of God through Christ" (Galatians 4:7).

"But you are a chosen generation, a royal priesthood, a holy nation, His own special people, that you may proclaim the praises of Him who called you out of darkness into His marvelous light" (1 Peter 2:9).

Wear your crown and your royal heritage in confidence, not in a prideful way, but in humility and love which is Jesus Christ. Knowing who God is and knowing who you are will help you to be confident in His love for you. In return, this knowledge will help you to continually let go and place things confidently in His hands to handle.

"Therefore if there is any consolation in Christ, if any comfort of love, if any fellowship of the Spirit, if any affection and mercy, fulfill my joy by being like-minded, having the same love, being of one accord, of one mind. Let

nothing be done through selfish ambition or conceit, but in lowliness of mind let each esteem others better than himself. Let each of you look out not only for his own interests, but also for the interests of others. *Let this mind be in you which was also in Christ Jesus,* who, being in the form of God, did not consider it robbery to be equal with God, but made Himself of no reputation, taking the form of a bondservant, and coming in the likeness of men. And being found in appearance as a man, He humbled Himself and became obedient to the point of death, even the death of the cross. Therefore God also has highly exalted Him and given Him the name which is above every name, hat at the name of Jesus every knee should bow, of those in heaven, and of those on earth, and of those under the earth, and that every tongue should confess that Jesus Christ is Lord, to the glory of God the Father" (Philippians 2:1–11).

Chapter 8
Baby Steps

When you learn to let go and begin to take possession of God's liberty, you will begin to step into His purpose and promises for your life. God will place people in your path—not necessarily Christians—but people who will help to propel you forward. When the Israelites left their bondage to the Egyptians, God granted them favor with the people so when they asked they Egyptians for provision for the journey they gave them what they asked for! "So, I will stretch out My hand and strike Egypt with all My wonders which I will do in its midst; and after that he will let you go. And I will give this people favor in the sight of the Egyptians; and it shall be, when you go, that you shall not go empty-handed. But every woman shall ask of her neighbor, namely, of her who dwells near her house, articles of silver, articles of gold, and clothing; and you shall put them on your sons and on your daughters. So, you shall plunder the Egyptians" (Exodus 3:20–22).

When the Israelites crossed over into the promised land, they came against the city of Jericho which was fortified by a mighty wall. They sent men to spy. They came to a house of a harlot. She had heard about them and hid them from the king's men who wanted to capture them. God can use anyone, anywhere. He can cause anyone He chooses to hear His voice. "The LORD will cause His glorious voice to be heard, And show the descent of His arm, With the indignation of His anger And the flame of a devouring fire, With scattering, tempest, and hailstones" (Isaiah 30:30).

When it is time for you to possess your breakthrough, your promises, your answered prayers, God will give you instructions. He will provide for the journey you are about to embark on, and He will lead the way. He has a great purpose for you and has blessings for you along the way. He has blessings for daily provision, wisdom, and spiritual blessings.

"Blessed be the God and Father of our Lord Jesus Christ, who has blessed us in Christ with every spiritual blessing in the heavenly places in Christ, just as He chose us in Him before the foundation of the world, that we should be holy and without blame before Him in love, having predestined us to adoption as sons by Jesus Christ to Himself, according to the good pleasure of His will, to the praise of the glory of His grace, by which He made us accepted in the Beloved. In Him we have redemption through His blood, the forgiveness of sins, according to the riches of His grace which He made to abound toward us in all wisdom and prudence, having made known to us the mystery of His will, according to His good pleasure which He purposed in Himself, that in the dispensation of the fullness of the times He might gather together in one all things in Christ, both which are in heaven and which are on earth—in Him. In Him also we have obtained an inheritance, being predestined according to the purpose of Him who works all things according to the counsel of His will, that we who first trusted in Christ should be to the praise of His glory. In Him you also trusted, after you heard the word of truth, the gospel of your salvation; in whom also, having believed, you were sealed with the Holy Spirit of promise, who is the guarantee of our inheritance until the redemption of the purchased possession, to the praise of His glory" (Ephesians 1:3–14).

Do not worry about making mistakes. He even has a way of turning those mistakes around for your good! He is God Almighty, and He is your Father! He will always make a way and finish what He starts in you if you do not give up. "And we know that all things work together for good to those who love God, to those who are the called according to His purpose" (Romans 8:28).

He has blessings for you on each journey you embark on with Him, but a gift is not a gift until you receive it and take possession of it. "Remember the word which Moses the servant of the LORD commanded you, saying, 'The LORD your God is giving you rest and is giving you this land'" (Joshua 1:13).

Stop being afraid of the unknown and dare to trust Him. Let go of control and the need to know things ahead of time before you step out. Take one baby step at a time and he will amaze you! Take possession of what He has called yours! "Every place on which the sole of your foot treads shall be yours: from the wilderness and Lebanon, from the river, the River Euphrates, even to the Western Sea, shall be your territory" (Deuteronomy 11:24).

Step by Step

Step by step You lead me. Step by step I follow.
You lead me in the everlasting way.

Though darkness may surround, the light of Your glory illuminates my path.

Darkness is not dark to You,
in childlike faith I follow.

Though darkness may surround; darkness is not dark to You.
The light of Your glory lights my way.

Step by step I follow.
You lead me in the way everlasting.

Step by step You lead me. Step by step I follow.
You lead me in the everlasting way.
You bore my sins. You wore my pain; in it I am healed.

By the cross You carried all my sins, all my pain and all my worries are nailed to it. So, step by step I follow.

You rose to glory and left life, liberty, and purity behind through Your Holy Spirit, so step by step I follow.

Step by step You lead me. Step by step I follow.
You lead me in the everlasting way until finally those steps lead me home.

Peace comes when we surrender. We need to stop trying to fit God into our plans and surrender our plans to Him. He will do a much better job. "Now to Him who is able to do exceedingly abundantly above all that we ask or think, according to the power that works in us" (Ephesians 3:20). Saying "Thy will be done" is so freeing once you start to live by those words.

When Paul (who was Saul until the Lord changed his name), was on his way to Damascus to have more Christians killed, the Lord blinded him, and he fell off his horse. The men that traveled with him led him all the way to Damascus. God provided the help he needed to see physically and spiritually. Sometimes the trials we face are simply God leading us on the road. These trials can open our eyes to something He is trying to teach us. God sent Ananias to Paul and healed his eyes. When he received his eyesight back, he also received his spiritual eyesight. He became a believer and wrote half of the New Testament.

Then there was Peter. Jesus had sent the disciples out ahead of him to Capernaum after a long day of teaching. Then Jesus came to them by walking on the water. Peter was the only one who called out to the Lord. The only one who sought his instruction.

"And Peter answered Him and said, 'Lord, if it is You, command me to come to You on the water.' So He said, 'Come.' And when Peter had come down out of the boat, he walked on the water to go to Jesus. But when he saw that the wind was boisterous, he was afraid; and beginning to sink he cried out, saying, 'Lord, save me!' And immediately Jesus stretched out His hand and caught him, and said to him, 'O you of little faith, why did you doubt?' And when they got into the boat, the wind ceased. Then those who were in the boat came and worshiped Him, saying, 'Truly You are the Son of God'"'" (Matthew 14:28–33).

Peter was the only one who got out of the boat. And when Paul took his eyes off Jesus and looked at the storm and became afraid, Jesus showed mercy and took hold of him. Peter grew afraid but at least he took a step and got out of the boat! You will never see wonderful things God has for you if you do not allow Him to take control. He will bless you, but the "Wow" moments will not happen unless you take a step. Take baby steps and give Him control of one thing at a time. He will amaze you and your faith will grow. As your faith grows it will help you to hand over another thing and another until you can finally say, "I surrender all."

Our prayers are answered, and His purpose fulfilled based on who God is, not us. Our only role is to not give up and keep believing, following, and obeying Him. He will lead. He will guide. He will inspire you and direct your path. He will place the right people in your path in His timing to help His purpose be fulfilled. "The LORD of hosts has sworn, saying, 'Surely, as I have thought, so it shall come to pass, And as I have purposed, so it shall stand'" (Isaiah 14:24).

God's promises are not based on our past mistakes or things we have done. His love is not based on our present actions. His purpose is fulfilled in and through us based on who He is and what He has already done for and through us and our continued faith in Him. Following Him, trusting him, helps us to move forward.

His promises are firm, and we need to trust Him and trust His Word and stand on His promises without wavering. Victory will happen as a result. Step out and find out what God has in store for you. You will be amazed! How can He amaze you if you do not let Him? Take it one step at a time. Learn to trust in His overwhelming love. Give yourself completely to Him. He will deliver you step by step, one issue at a time. God will heal your heart and help you to trust Him so you can finally let go completely and surrender all. "And the LORD your

God will drive out those nations before you little by little; you will be unable to destroy them at once, lest the beasts of the field become *too* numerous for you" (Deuteronomy 7:22).

Taking baby steps means letting go of one issue at a time and giving those issues over to God. We must surrender those things completely to Him without worry. We must trust Him to answer our prayers, in His time and way. It took time for me to let go of all my fears. I did it this same way—step by step. And I included words of positive affirmation each time. This helped bring my faith to life in my heart. I had to say, sometimes over and over, "I trust You, Jesus." I would also use the promises I found in the Bible that had to do with what I was praying. God's words are spirit and life. As He spoke and things came to be, I felt that spirit and life inside me. This is because His Spirit lives in me. His same Spirit that created the world will bring the promises we speak over our life and that of our loved ones to life as well. "It is the Spirit who gives life; the flesh profits nothing. The words that I speak to you are spirit, and they are life" (John 6:63).

When you speak these promises out loud, your heart hears and gives you hope and faith. "So then faith comes by hearing, and hearing by the word of God." (Romans 10:17).

Then you will experience all that He has for you and everything He promises will come to pass!

"Behold, this day I am going the way of all the earth. And you know in all your hearts and in all your souls that not one thing has failed of all the good things which the LORD your God spoke concerning you. All have come to pass for you; not one word of them has failed. Therefore it shall come to pass, that as all the good things have come upon you which the LORD your God promised you, so the LORD will bring upon you all harmful things, until He has destroyed you from this good land which the LORD your God has given you" (Joshua 23:14–15).

Chapter 9
I Believe! Letting Go

Letting go of the chains, the fear, worry, and unbelief which keep you frozen and bound will lead to freedom. Freedom only happens by trusting God. When you finally shed all that weight and believe what and who God says about you, you will have freedom.

Once you begin to let go, step by step, issue by issue, and you feel that liberty within, you will want to keep going. You will want to keep experiencing the overwhelming joy you receive when you let go and surrender all and trust God completely.

"Praise the LORD! Blessed is the man who fears the LORD, Who greatly delights in His commandments. His descendants will be mighty on earth; The generation of the upright will be blessed. Wealth and riches will be in his house, And his righteousness endures forever. Unto the upright there arises light in the darkness; He is gracious, and full of compassion, and righteous. A good man deals graciously and lends; He will guide his affairs with discretion. Surely he will never be shaken; The righteous will be in everlasting remembrance. He will not be afraid of evil tidings; His heart is steadfast, trusting in the Lord. His heart is established; He will not be afraid, Until he sees his desire upon his enemies. He has dispersed abroad; He has given to the poor; His righteousness endures forever; His horn will be exalted with honor. The wicked will see it and be grieved; He will gnash his teeth and melt away; The desire of the wicked shall perish" (Psalm 112).

I can finally say, after many years, "I trust you, Lord, with all of my heart." It took many years of constant worry and fear, when it came to letting go of my oldest son. He had so much depression that led to a life of drugs and life living on the streets. That was in part due to losing my youngest son, I was afraid of losing him as well. But you cannot ride the wings of the Holy Spirit until you shake off the weight of sin, worry, unbelief, anger, and all those negative emotions.

"Therefore we also, since we are surrounded by so great a cloud of witnesses, let us lay aside every weight, and the sin which so easily ensnares us, and let us run with endurance the race that is set before us, looking unto Jesus, the author and finisher of our faith, who for the joy that was set before Him endured the cross, despising the shame, and has sat down at the right hand of the throne of God. For consider Him who endured such hostility from sinners against Himself, lest you become weary and discouraged in your souls" (Hebrews 12:1–3).

"But you have not so learned Christ, if indeed you have heard Him and have been taught by Him, as the truth is in Jesus: that you put off, concerning your former conduct, the old man which grows corrupt according to the deceitful lusts, and be renewed in the spirit of your mind, and that you put on the new man which was created according to God, in true righteousness and holiness. Therefore, putting away lying, 'Let each one of you speak truth with his neighbor,' for we are members of one another. 'Be angry, and do not sin': do not let the sun go down on your wrath, nor give place to the devil. Let him who stole steal no longer, but rather let him labor, working with his hands what is good, that he may have something to give him who has need. Let no corrupt word proceed out of your mouth, but what is good for necessary edification, that it may impart grace to the hearers. And do not grieve the Holy Spirit of God, by whom you were sealed for the day of redemption. Let all bitterness, wrath, anger, clamor, and evil speaking be put away from you, with all malice. And be kind to one another, tenderhearted, forgiving one another, even as God in Christ forgave you" (Ephesians 4:20–32).

Letting go is surrendering all to the Lord and is dying to self. "For to me, to live is Christ, and to die is gain" (Philippians 1:21).

I Died Today

Lifeless in Your hands, You carry me.
I am dead to the world and to my flesh
that You may live free in me.

I have fought and wrestled against the struggles
in my heart, wanting all the pain to be free from me.

The answers to my pain You already knew.
There was only one thing that I needed to do.

Yet I struggled on, trying in my own way and
praying in desperation. The fight continued on;
my heart truly broken. I cry out, "Please, God,
show me Your way!"

You knew the way and were patient with my
stubborn heart; fighting for its own way and failing
to see it Yours.

Weary from the pain and the trials that wore me out;
I fall lifeless into Your hands. The path has broken
my heart.

I finally died today. My will inside me gone.
It's buried with my pain and in Your hands I lay.

My heart cries out, "I'm tired, Lord, there's no
more fight, my heart struggles no more."

To my amazement, the peace I sought finally came.
When to my will I died, and I called to You and gave myself.
My heart will never be the same.

That was the way all along. For God is great and His way is best. We must die to self and seek His grace.
In us, let His glory be revealed that we may see His face.

He'll wait patiently to hear us say, "Lord, not my will, but Thy will be done." His peace will come and you will never be the same. When in your heart His presence known; you will shine; His glory known in Jesus name.

As a mom, I do not know if I could have done what the mother of Moses did when she floated him down the Nile River to save his life. A new king came to power in Egypt and saw that the Hebrews were becoming numerous and commanded the Hebrew midwives to kill all the male newborn women. They could not do it but made excuses.

The mother of Moses his him for three months. When she could not hide him any longer, she floated him down the Nile River in hopes of saving his life. She hoped someone would find him and raise him.

"And a man of the house of Levi went and took as wife a daughter of Levi. So the woman conceived and bore a son. And when she saw that he was a beautiful child, she hid him three months. But when she could no longer hide him, she took an ark of bulrushes for him, daubed it with asphalt and pitch, put the child in it, and laid it in the reeds by the river's bank. And his sister stood afar off, to know what would be done to him. Then the daughter of Pharaoh came down to bathe at the river. And her maidens walked along the riverside; and when she saw the ark among the reeds, she sent her maid to get it. And when she opened it, she saw the child, and behold, the baby wept. So she had compassion on him, and said, 'This is one of the Hebrews' children.' Then his sister said to Pharaoh's daughter, 'Shall I go and call a nurse for you from the Hebrew women, that she may nurse the child for you?' And Pharaoh's daughter said to her, 'Go.' So the maiden went and called the child's mother. Then Pharaoh's daughter said to her, 'Take this child away and nurse him for me, and I will give you your wages.' So the woman took the child and nursed him. And the child grew, and she brought him to Pharaoh's daughter, and he became her son. So she called his name Moses, saying, 'Because I drew him out of the water'"" (Exodus 2:1–10).

Sending her son down the river had to take a lot of faith that God would protect him. God honored that faith as He saved Moses's life. Moses would eventually be the one God used to deliver His people from bondage to the Egyptians. "The fear of the LORD leads to life, And he who has it will abide in satisfaction; He will not be visited with evil" (Proverbs 19:23).

Besides the story of Moses, I am sure you have heard of the story of Abraham and Isaac. Isaac was Abraham's only son bore to him by his wife Sarah when they were both in their old age. Abraham was 100 years old! The Lord promised Abraham a son when he was 75 years old and Sarah was 65. They waited twenty-five years until Isaac was born. He was the promised son born to them in their old age.

God had called him out of his land to go to Canaan and Abraham obeyed. He had a few mishaps along the way, but as humans, don't we all? Abraham continued to obey the Lord. God told him he would have a son when Abraham told God that he had no heir. "And behold, the word of the Lord came to him, saying, 'This one shall not be your heir, but one who will come from your own body shall be your heir.' Then He brought him outside and said, 'Look now toward heaven, and count the stars if you are able to number them.' And He said to him, 'So shall your descendants be.' And he believed in the Lord, and He accounted it to him for righteousness" (Genesis 15:4–6).

Then, after finally receiving a son, at 100 years old, God commands him to offer him up as a sacrifice! God made a covenant with Abraham that he would make his descendants as numerous as the stars in the heaven. With that covenant, He made him a promise of his first-born son with Sarah. The covenant also had a condition, that every male child would be circumcised.

The Lord told Abraham to offer his only son as an offering. "Then He said, "Take now your son, your only *son* Isaac, whom you love, and go to the land of Moriah, and offer him there as a burnt offering on one of the mountains of which I shall tell you." (Genesis 22:2)   Abraham obeyed God; what a hard thing to do! I do not think I could have done that!

"Do not lay a hand on the lad or do anything to him; for now I know that you fear God, since you have not withheld your son, your only son, from Me.' Then Abraham lifted his eyes and looked, and there behind him was a ram caught in a thicket by its horns. So Abraham went and took the ram, and offered it up for a burnt offering instead of his son. And Abraham called the name of the place, The-Lord-Will-Provide; as it is said to this day, 'In the Mount of the Lord it shall be provided.' Then the Angel of the Lord called to Abraham a second time out of heaven, and said: 'By Myself I have sworn, says the Lord, because you have done this thing, and have not withheld your son, your only son—blessing

I will bless you, and multiplying I will multiply your descendants as the stars of the heaven and as the sand which is on the seashore; and your descendants shall possess the gate of their enemies. In your seed all the nations of the earth shall be blessed, because you have obeyed My voice'" (Genesis 22:12–18).

Did you notice what he said, "The boy and I will go over there to worship, and then we will return to you." He totally trusted God and God blessed him for his overwhelming faith!

What overwhelming faith! Do you want that kind of faith? I do not think I want to prove it in that way, but I want that kind of faith. That kind of faith takes effort. One step at a time as you let go of one issue and give it over to God, your faith will grow as you let Him amaze you as only He can do. "Now to Him who is able to do exceedingly abundantly above all that we ask or think, according to the power that works in us" (Ephesians 3:20).

Let Go and Let God

God in his faithfulness never changes.
His love is constant.
He doesn't move, we do.

If in His love our trials break us,
It is simply to mold and to change us.

Let go and let God.
He loves you and will not
fail or forsake you.

The change will bring trust and faith
and in you love, peace and joy
it will produce.

Let go and let God.
His love is constant
His plan never fails, we do.

He is always faithful
His love is true.
If you let Him, He will move you.

Let go and let God!

Chapter 10
Drinking from the Well

Once you learn to let go, then it will be time to experience the freedom that comes with that. Then you can watch and see God continually amaze you. It is when you finally believe—when you can believe without needing a sign—that you will be ready to soar. You will be ready to soar on the wings of the Holy Spirit. "But those who wait on the LORD Shall renew their strength; They shall mount up with wings like eagles, They shall run and not be weary, They shall walk and not faint" (Isaiah 40:31).

Broken Wings

With Broken Wings I worship you.
You give me strength and, in my spirit,
Your grace flows through.

Fly High! Fly High!
With Broken Wings, Fly High!
Fly High! My spirit sings! Fly High!

Fly High! with Broken Wings.
If Jesus Christ is your King,
you'll know the song my spirit sings!

Fly High! Fly High!
With Broken Wings, Fly High!
Fly High! My spirit sings! Fly High!

Fly High, up through the skies.
Sing the joy my Savior brings.
Fly High! Fly High!
My voice is raised in praise, Fly High!

Fly High! Fly High!
With Broken Wings, Fly High!
Fly High! My spirit sings!
The Savior Reigns!
Up on His throne so High,
Fly High!

The very first freedom we receive is when we believe in Jesus Christ that He is the Son of God and that He laid down His life as an atonement for our sins. He died, we believe, and receive His Spirit. Then we receive the eternal salvation of our souls. "For this is My blood of the new covenant, which is shed for many for the remission of sins" (Matthew 26:28). This is a covenant between God and us with a promise of salvation and the condition that we must believe and receive.

"For God so loved the world that He gave His only begotten Son, that whoever believes in Him should not perish but have everlasting life. For God did not send His Son into the world to condemn the world, but that the world through Him might be saved. He who believes in Him is not condemned, but he who does not believe is condemned already, because he has not believed in the name of the only begotten Son of God" (John 3:16–18).

"But as many as received Him, to them He gave the right to become children of God, to those who believe in His name" (John 1:12).

We are free from the power of sin. We still have a choice, free will, but with the Holy Spirit within us, and our new love for Him, we will not want to sin any longer. The Holy Spirit helps us and guides us through life.

"For if we have been united together in the likeness of His death, certainly we also shall be in the likeness of His resurrection, knowing this, that our old man was crucified with Him, that the body of sin might be done away with, that we should no longer be slaves of sin. For he who has died has been freed from sin. Now if we died with Christ, we believe that we shall also live with Him, knowing that Christ, having been raised from the dead, dies no more. Death no longer has dominion over Him. For the death that He died, He died to sin once for all; but the life that He lives, He lives to God. Likewise you also, reckon yourselves to be dead indeed to sin, but alive to God in Christ Jesus our Lord" (Romans 6:5-11).

The death we die when we are saved is a spiritual death. We die to our sin nature and are born again in Christ. "Jesus answered and said to him, 'Most assuredly, I say to you, unless one is born again, he cannot see the kingdom of God'" (John 3:3).

When we receive the Holy Spirit into our hearts, we are made new!

"I will give you a new heart and put a new spirit within you; I will take the heart of stone out of your flesh and give you a heart of flesh" (Ezekiel 36:26).

"Therefore, if anyone is in Christ, he is a new creation; old things have passed away; behold, all things have become new" (2 Corinthians 5:17).

Each time we let something go and give it over to God, He will answer in a bigger and better way! Afterall, He is the Creator. "For thus says the Lord, Who created the heavens, Who is God, Who formed the earth and made it, Who has established it, Who did not create in vain, Who formed it to be inhabited: 'I am the LORD, and there is no other.'" (Isaiah 45:18).

If God would send His Son to die a death that we deserve, just to spare us so we would have an eternal home with Him, how much more will He answer our prayers in a great way?

"He who did not spare His own Son, but delivered Him up for us all, how shall He not with Him also freely give us all things?" (Romans 8:32).

The love of God is so great for us—He did not want to lose us. He is love and all love comes from Him. "Beloved, let us love one another, for love is of God; and everyone who loves is born of God and knows God. He who does not love does not know God, for God is love. In this the love of God was manifested toward us, that God has sent His only begotten Son into the world, that we might live through Him. In this is love, not that we loved God, but that He loved us and sent His Son to be the propitiation for our sins. Beloved, if God so loved us, we also ought to love one another. No one has seen God at any time. If we love one another, God abides in us, and His love has been perfected in us. By this we know that we abide in Him, and He in us, because He has given us of His Spirit. And we have seen and testify that the Father has sent the Son as Savior of the world" (1 John 4:7–14).

We have all sinned against Him, and He still chose to die for us. "But God demonstrates His own love toward us, in that while we were still sinners, Christ died for us" (Romans 5:8).

Do you really understand just how painful it was for God to give his only Son? Jesus was made flesh that He could understand us, so the pain He felt was real. "Inasmuch then as the children have partaken of flesh and blood, He Himself likewise shared in the same, that through death He might destroy him who had the power of death, that is, the devil, and release those who through fear of death were all their lifetime subject to bondage. For indeed He does not give aid to angels, but He does give aid to the seed of Abraham. Therefore, in all things He had to be made like His brethren, that He might be a merciful and faithful High Priest in things pertaining to God, to make propitiation for the sins of the people. For in that He Himself has suffered, being tempted, He is able to aid those who are tempted" (Hebrews 2:14–18).

Jesus was beaten so badly it says that He was beyond human likeness. He was spit on and mocked and He still chose to die for us! "Behold, My Servant shall deal prudently; He shall be exalted and extolled and be very high. Just as many were astonished at you, So His visage was marred more than any man, And His form more than the sons of men; So shall He sprinkle many nations. Kings shall shut their mouths at Him; For what had not been told them they shall see, And what they had not heard they shall consider" (Isaiah 52:13–15). That is love! "Greater love has no one than this, than to lay down one's life for his friends" (John 15:13). Do not doubt that God will answer your prayers. Let go and soar!

Abraham believed God and gave birth to a son at the age of one hundred and became the father of many nations.

Joseph continued to have faith even though his brothers threw him into a pit to die, and then sold him into slavery. From there, he was accused wrongly and thrown into prison. You will not read one time in his story of Joseph complaining. Finally, he was promoted to a position in the palace.

Daniel and his friends would not eat the foods of the land or bow to the god's of the land. His friends were thrown into a fire and still they did not deny God. They were promoted to a position in the palace.

Esther, an orphan, was taken from her uncle's home and forced to enter servitude to the king. She did not complain. She was made queen.

Ruth lost her husband and left her homeland and her family. She worked hard gleaning the fields for leftovers without complaining. She married the owner of the fields and became part of the lineage of Jesus Christ.

Paul was blinded and knocked off his horse in order to open his eyes to the truth of Jesus Christ. After receiving his eyesight back, he did not complain. He regained his strength and then immediately got up and went to the disciples. He encouraged new believers with his letters and wrote half of the New Testament.

Mary let go of what people would think about her becoming pregnant and gave birth to Jesus Christ, the Son of God!

When you stay close to God and keep your eyes focused on Him, He will direct you to stay on His path. You will continually draw from the wells of His goodness to give you the strength, peace, and faith you need. "Therefore with joy you will draw water From the wells of salvation" (Isaiah 12:3). What does God have in store for you? To find out, you need to step out and drink from the well of His goodness.

"They shall utter the memory of Your great goodness, And shall sing of your righteousness" (Psalm 145:7).

On the Wings of an Eagle

When the problems I face are
too much to bear, I know that He cares.
In my weakness, He's my strength.
He lifts me up on the Wings of an Eagle
and on His love my heart
feels lighter than air.

On the Wings of an Eagle
we soar through the air,
through the clouds we ride
and now my problems seem so small.
In my weakness, He's my strength
His love will not let me fall.

When I feel overwhelmed
He's the one I run to,
the only one I need.
In His strength, I can carry on.
He guides me through life
On the Wings of an Eagle
His love carries me.

Epilogue

Freedom, how sweet it is indeed! Once you have learned that letting go of the fear, worry, and unbelief is actually resolving the issue, you will be able to rest in your spirit. "Come to Me, all you who labor and are heavy laden, and I will give you rest" (Matthew 11:28).

Our Lord promises in His word that He will sustain us and take care of us as we cast every burden on to Him. "Cast your burden on the LORD, And He shall sustain you; He shall never permit the righteous to be moved" (Psalm 55:22).

Giving your cares over to the Lord is allowing Him to carry you through your problems and into victory! "Even to your old age, I am He, And even to gray hairs I will carry you! I have made, and I will bear; Even I will carry, and will deliver you" (Isaiah 46:4). Picture yourself in God's hands, much like being carried through the air in a hot air balloon. Allow God to carry you in the same way. This will happen every time you let go and give your troubles and your prayers to Him, completely without doubt or fear.

If the problem is too much for you, then it is not yours to bear, but our Father's. "Blessed be the LORD, Who daily loads us with benefits, The God of our salvation! Selah" (Psalm 68:19).

Now that you have learned this, step out and find out how exhilarating it is to cast your cares upon the Lord! This is like someone coming along and telling you they are taking care of a bill you cannot afford to pay. You would truly rejoice! The Father wants to do that with every problem you face. Won't you let Him? Learning to let go will allow you to soar your way through each trial. Each time you pray and ask the Father for wisdom, He will answer; "If any of you lacks wisdom, let him ask of God, who gives to all liberally and without reproach, and it will be given to him" (James 1:5). As you go through each trial, worry begins to set in. Ask, "Father, what are you trying to teach me in this? What lesson do you want me to learn? What are you trying to draw out of me? What direction should I go and how do I handle this?" He will show you. He will give you the answer. "These things I have written to you who believe in the name of the Son of God, that you may know that you have eternal life, and that you may continue to believe in the name of the Son of God. Now this is the confidence that we have in Him, that if we ask anything according to His will, He hears us. And if we know that He hears us, whatever we ask, we know that we have the petitions that we have asked of Him" (1 John 5:13–15).

Step by step as you learn to let go and give your troubles to the over to the Lord, your faith will grow each time He answers and takes care of the problem. Out of all the disciples who walked with Jesus daily and saw Him perform every miracle, it was only one who got out of the boat: Peter. He may have taken his eyes off Jesus and looked at the storm, but at least he got out of the boat! He experienced an amazing feat! How will you ever experience the greatness of our God if you do not follow Him onto the water or into the storm?

He tells us in His word that He is our help in times of trouble. Do you call on Him to help? "God is our refuge and strength, A very present help in trouble" (Psalm 46:1).

You can let go and let God carry you through your troubles and through life! You can do this!

"The LORD your God, who goes before you, He will fight for you, according to all He did for you in Egypt before your eyes, and in the wilderness where you saw how the LORD your God carried you, as a man carries his son, in all the way that you went until you came to this place" (Deuteronomy 1:30–31).

Carry Me

Carry me when my trials overwhelm me and my load gets too much to bear. I run to You and seek Your face; Your love is always there.

I will worship You and seek Your saving grace
I will worship You and always seek Your face.

Surrendered to Your love, I'm carried by your grace. Your strength holds me up; Your love will never fail or forsake.

Carry me, O Lord; I'm surrendered to Your mercy and Your grace.
Carry me, O Lord; Your love will hold me up and the forgiveness through Your blood has given my heart a new face.

Carry me, O Lord, through life's hills and valleys, good times and bad.
Carry me, O Lord, I'm surrendered to Your grace.
In repentance all my sins are erased.
Your glory I will always seek because I'm surrendered to Your grace.

Carry me, O Lord, into the heights of the heavens above and into the depths of Your love.
Surrendered to Your will, I'm carried by Your grace.

Your strength holds me up and Your love will never fail or forsake.
Carry me, O Lord, I'm surrendered to Your grace.
I will worship You and always seek Your face.

Special Invitation

I cannot close this book without giving you the awesome privilege of becoming a child of God, a chance to have every wrong made right and every sin washed away. If you have never asked Jesus into your heart, or maybe you did but you were never sincere, please pray this *Invitation to Salvation* prayer. It will be the best thing you have ever done.

Invitation to Salvation Prayer

Dear Almighty Father in heaven, I know that I am a sinner and I ask Your forgiveness of all my sins. I want to make You the Lord of my life and I want to serve You all the days of my life. I believe that Jesus Christ died on the cross for my sins. Thank You so much for loving me and waiting on me to come to the knowledge of the truth! Thank You for my salvation. Please help me and guide me in learning Your Word so I can be a light to the world. Please, Jesus, come into my heart, and baptize me with Your Holy Spirit. I thank You and praise Your Holy Name and ask all this in the name of Jesus Christ our Lord. Amen.

****

After you do this, find a good church to go to if you do not have one already. Fellowshipping with other Christians will help you on your new walk in Christ. It is also a place to worship God and learn more about Him. Also, tell someone! You must confess! This should be the happiest day of your life because you now know that your eternal home is in heaven! I think that is the best life insurance any one can have and it is free! "That if you confess with your mouth the Lord Jesus and believe in your heart that God has raised Him from the dead, you will be saved. For with the heart one believes unto righteousness, and with the mouth confession is made unto salvation" (Romans 10:9–10).

Congratulations and welcome to the family of God!

GOD LOVES YOU!

"I have loved you with an everlasting love; Therefore with lovingkindness I have drawn you." (Jeremiah 31:3)

"God our Savior, who desires all men to be saved and to come to the knowledge of the truth." (1 Timothy 2:3–4)

He will not knock on the door to your heart forever, Judgement Day will come. Will you let Him in?

"Behold, I stand at the door and knock. If anyone hears My voice and opens the door, I will come in to him and dine with him, and he with Me." (Revelation 3:20)

"When once the Master of the house has risen up and shut the door, and you begin to stand outside and knock at the door, saying, 'Lord, Lord, open for us,' and He will answer and say to you, 'I do not know you, where you are from.'" (Luke 13:25)

Jesus is the only way to God.

"I am the way, the truth, and the life. No one comes to the Father except through Me." (John 14:6)

"Most assuredly, I say to you, unless one is born again, he cannot see the kingdom of God." (John 3:3)

And you must make Him Lord of your life.

"No one can serve two masters." (Matthew 6:24)

"Not everyone who says to Me, 'Lord, Lord', shall enter the kingdom of heaven, but only he who does the will of My Father in heaven." (Matthew 7:21)

We must leave our old ways behind.

"And if a house is divided against itself, that house cannot stand." (Mark 3:25)

You cannot live according to the flesh and desires of the sinful nature and expect to have Jesus in your heart. He is holy. He is love. Love and hate cannot exist together.

"But you have not so learned Christ, if indeed you have heard Him and have been taught by Him, as the truth is in Jesus: that you put off, concerning your former conduct, the old man which grows corrupt according to the deceitful lusts, and be renewed in the spirit of your mind, and that you put on the new man which was created according to God, in true righteousness and holiness." (Ephesians 4:20-24)

God gives you the ability to do His will. He knows it is hard.
"I can do all things through Christ who strengthens me." (Philippians 4:13)

"For all have sinned and fall short of the glory of God." (Romans 3:23)

"If we confess our sins, He is faithful and just to forgive us our sins and to cleanse us from all unrighteousness." (I John 1:9)

"But as many as received Him, to them He gave the right to become children of God, to those who believe in His name." (John 1:12)

"For with the heart one believes unto righteousness, and with the mouth confession is made unto salvation." (Romans 10:10)

Then after you confess and ask forgiveness and receive Jesus into your heart, you must testify (tell someone) and be baptized. In this, God is glorified, and others might be saved by your example.

"Therefore do not be ashamed of the testimony of our Lord." (II Timothy 1:8)

"There is also an antitype which now saves us—baptism (not the removal of the filth of the flesh, but the answer of a good conscience toward God), through the resurrection of Jesus Christ." (I Peter 3:21)

Other Books by Sandra Lott

Jeremy's Journey: From a Prison Cell to a Healed Heart
Deep Waters Within
Hannah: From Barren to Blossom
Step by Step into a Deeper Walk in Christ
Ride the Wind
An Eagle's Flight
A Princess in Waiting
God's Love
My Father's Eyes: Seeing Yourself Through the Eyes of Love
I'm Saved! Where Do I Go from Here?
The Day Hope Was Born: God's Gift of Love
The Holy Spirit and the Baptism of the Holy Spirit
Repairing Broken Walls: Restoring Joy & Peace-The Book
Repairing Broken Walls: Restoring Joy & Peace-The Study Guide
Abide in Me: A Seven Week Study on the Blessings of God's Presence

Children's Books

The Sheep that Went Astray
Naomi's Joy
Tim & Gerald Ray Series: The Wind has a Voice
Tim & Gerald Ray Series: How Did He Get in There?
Tim & Gerald Ray Series: Let's Go Swimming
Tim & Gerald Ray Series: A Light in the Sky

Author Sandra Lott was born and raised in Texas and is the author of Deep Waters Within, Ride the Wind, God's Love and My Father's Eyes: Seeing Yourself through the Eyes of Love and more. She has learned about the love and faithfulness of God through the death of her sixteen-year-old son and many other hardships. Through His love and comfort she has drawn close to the Father's love and has developed a passion for studying the Bible. That deep devotion to God in turn has given her the desire to help others grow in their understanding of the love of God and to grow spiritually.

Milton Keynes UK
Ingram Content Group UK Ltd.
UKHW032149170324
439604UK00012B/1623